YORK NOTES

General Editors: Professor A.N. Jeffares *University of Stirling*) & Professor Suheil Bushrui (*American University of Beirut*)

Bernard Shaw

PYGMALION

dies,

LONGMAN
YORK PRESS

11318/9
822-

The illustrations of The Globe Playhouse are from
The Globe Restored in Theatre: A Way of Seeing by
Walter C. Hodges, published by Oxford University
Press. © Oxford University Press

YORK PRESS
Immeuble Esseily, Place Riad Solh, Beirut.

LONGMAN GROUP UK LIMITED
Longman House, Burnt Mill, Harlow,
Essex CM20 2JE, England
and Associated Companies throughout the world.

© Librairie du Liban 1980

First published 1980
Reprinted 1989

ISBN 0-582-02299-1

Produced by Longman Group (FE) Ltd
Printed in Hong Kong

Contents

Part 1

Introduction

Shaw and Ireland

The richness and variety of English literature, especially dramatic literature, owes much to Irish writers. George Bernard Shaw belongs to this company. He was born on 26 July 1856, in Dublin, the city which was to become the capital of the Irish Free State. Ireland still had a largely rural economy and a feudal social organisation: the population was mostly divisible into peasants and landlords, the latter often absentees from their estates, living in Dublin or England. The terrible famines of the 1840s had left a lasting mark: a million Irishmen had died of starvation and the other hardships of extreme poverty, and there had been a mass emigration to America. Right to the end of the nineteenth century and beyond, Ireland had little to offer the hopeful and ambitious. Some stayed, or returned from America, and gradually built a political movement out of romantic patriotism, demanding Home Rule and independence from England. For many others Ireland remained a country to leave, if possible; and Shaw was among these. At the age of twenty he followed his mother and sisters to London and made his home in England for the rest of his life.

One reason for this move was the uneasy social position of the Shaw family in Ireland. The population of Dublin was mainly Roman Catholic in religion and associated Protestantism with the wealthy governing class (traditionally known as the Protestant Ascendancy), on the one hand, and with the more industrial Northern province of Ulster, on the other. Both these groups were pro-English for various reasons. The Shaws were Protestant, the family having long ago gone from Scotland to Ireland; yet they were far from wealthy. Although G.B. Shaw's father was only an unsuccessful corn-dealer, he—and his wife even more—claimed to belong to the gentry, or small land-owner class, and they thought themselves superior to the petty tradespeople and artisans among whom they lived. Their son learnt to see Irish Catholics as ignorant and superstitious as well as poor and coarse-mannered. The path to a belief in equality was not simple and easy for him.

Relationship with mother and father

G.B. Shaw was never called by his first name of George, which he shared with his father. George Carr Shaw not only failed in business, but offended his intensely self-respecting wife by becoming a habitual drinker and being seen drunk in public. In reaction, his son never drank alcohol and added vegetarianism to this asceticism. Bernard Shaw adored his mother and seems to have adopted her rather contemptuous attitude towards his father. Yet it was from his father that he inherited his sense of humour, his scepticism about romance or high ideals or pretentiousness of every kind, and his feeling that nothing, not even religion, was too sacred to be laughed at. He claimed that it was horror at his father's degradation that led him to repress his emotional nature and adopt the detachment needful for the art of comedy. But his mother was an emotionally detached woman, appearing coolly indifferent to her son, who felt himself unloved and neglected in a household where his sisters were given more of Mrs Shaw's attention. (The younger sister died before reaching maturity; the elder, Lucy, took up a stage career as a singer in light opera.) Though she did not teach him or have him taught music, Mrs Shaw's passion for music communicated itself to her son and stayed with him all his life. She was herself a talented amateur singer who performed a good deal in public, and for a time the eccentric teacher who trained her voice and conducted the concerts in which she sang, George John Vandaleur Lee, lived with the family. When he went to London in the hope of advancing himself professionally, Mrs Shaw followed with her daughters, leaving her son and husband behind. After two years of working as a clerk in Dublin, Bernard left his job and followed her.

Early struggles in London

Mrs Shaw made a living by teaching music, while her son was without regular work and dependent on her for ten years. He had had little continuous or systematic education and did not go to a university. During these years he educated himself by reading widely, going to public lectures and joining some of the debating societies then flourishing in London. He developed an ability to speak in public and, as time passed, he made the acquaintance of a number of people who were to be influential in the shaping of his career. He also occupied himself in writing novels, though he did not succeed in getting them published. William Archer, who was a journalist, social reformer, translator and champion of the great Norwegian dramatist, Ibsen, got Shaw his first journalistic appointment, as art critic to *The World* in 1886. This led to six years of music criticism, first for the new mass-circulation newspaper, *The Star* (Shaw wrote under the pseudonym of 'Corno di Bassetto'), then for *The World*. It is now generally recognised that in these reviews Shaw's knowledge and judgement as well as the liveliness of his writing raised the whole standard of music criticism in England.

Politics

On his own evidence, Shaw had already been converted to Socialism in 1882, when he heard a lecture by Henry George, author of *Progress and Poverty*, and he followed this up by reading a translation of the first volume of Marx's *Capital*. He became a street-corner orator for the Marxist Social Democratic Federation, which brought him into contact with William Morris, the artist and craftsman whose theories became influential across Europe, and with Marx's daughter, Eleanor, among others. But in 1884 he and Sidney Webb, who was to be a lifelong friend, joined the recently formed Fabian Society. Together with Webb's extremely able wife, Beatrice, they were to make this Society a powerhouse of ideas, based on research, which they endeavoured to pass on to the parliamentary parties (Tory and, more particularly, Liberal, before the emergence of the Labour Party). Shaw's experience in a street demonstration in 1887, when the crowds were easily routed by the police, convinced him that Socialism had no chance of success through revolution in England at that time. The way had to be prepared by hard planning, patient teaching and reform by parliamentary means wherever possible.

The Fabians formed a middle-class intelligentsia detached from the trade union movement. They were effective in promoting some of the main advances in social legislation in Britain in the first half of this century and could claim to be the architects of the Welfare State established by the Labour government after the second world war. Though his views underwent modification in detail, Shaw remained loyal to Fabian principles to the end of his life, and his major works of political education, *The Intelligent Woman's Guide to Socialism and Capitalism* (1928) and *Everybody's Political What's What?* (1944), were thoroughly Fabian in their nature and tendency. He was involved with the Webbs in founding a famous journal, *The New Statesman*, and in establishing the London School of Economics.

Ibsenism and feminism

In 1890 Shaw was asked to talk about Henrik Ibsen in one of a series of lectures on 'Socialism in Contemporary Literature', arranged by the Fabian Society. He later expanded and published his lecture as *The Quintessence of Ibsenism*. The context in which it was originally given partly accounts for the over-emphasis on social criticism in Ibsen's plays and the neglect of their poetic qualities for which Ibsen scholars from William Archer onwards have blamed Shaw. In particular, he presented Ibsen as an enemy of idealism, intent on destroying illusions and revealing the truth about society. Ibsen's *A Doll's House* had scandalised European audiences by its attack on conventional bourgeois marriage. His *Ghosts* was reported to be even more shocking, and English intellectuals were eager to have it performed in London. Under the conditions of theatrical censorship then prevailing, there was no chance of public presentation of a play that referred to such taboo subjects (unmentionable in ordinary or polite society) as venereal disease and incest—apart from the fact that Ibsen in questioning the value of the family was challenging the whole basis of Western society. So a club was formed, calling itself the Independent Theatre, and a production of *Ghosts* was arranged for its members in 1891. It caused a storm of protest in the newspapers and divided literary and fashionable society into conservative Ibsen-haters and progressive Ibsenites.

In particular, the growing band of campaigners for Women's Rights saw Ibsen as a champion of their cause. In the later nineteenth century, progressives concentrated on changing the laws to give women more personal freedom, allowing them to hold and manage property, to separate from their husbands on due cause, and to have a voice in the upbringing of their children. They also favoured the trend, among middle-class women, towards higher education and employment outside the home. It was at the beginning of this century, especially with the founding of the Women's Social and Political Union in 1903, that the women's campaign became militant and concentrated on a demand for political power, specifically the right to vote.

As a socialist Shaw certainly supported the emancipation of women, but his private attitude on this issue is not easy to define. One clue to it was his statement that his play *Candida* (1894) was an English version of *A Doll's House*, showing that in England the man, not the woman, was the doll within the marriage relationship. It would be a mistake to connect this view, and the long series of dominating women characters in his plays, exclusively with his personal family experience. It is at least equally a reflection on an ideal of woman widely held in the Victorian period: 'The hand that rocks the cradle rules the world' was a popular summing up of the enormous power that women as mothers, confined to the home, were supposed to exert indirectly as shapers of character and guardians of morality, in the age of imperialist expansion. One of Shaw's best known plays, *Man and Superman* (1903), borrows ideas from the German philosophers Schopenhauer (1788–1860) and Nietzsche (1844–1900) who saw the female Will struggling against the male power of Intellect. Elsewhere he mocks at old-fashioned sentimentalists who want a society divided into the extremes of 'womanly women' and 'manly men'. In fact, he seems to have been working out his ideas about women and their place in society throughout most of his novels and plays, and it is unsafe to generalise about them.

The theatre as Shaw knew it

Shaw had developed the habit of theatre-going in Dublin where, for very little money, he had been able to see a wide variety of entertainment, much of it rather old-fashioned by London standards. He went to operas, performances of Shakespeare, sentimental melodramas (a lower-class version of tragedy, accompanied by background music that worked on the audiences' feelings), comic burlesques, pantomimes and farces. As long as they were well done, he enjoyed even the least intellectual forms of entertainment: the physical, knockabout humours of farce; the performances of clowns in the harlequinades, or pantomimes. When he saw the classic plays of Shakespeare, they were drastically cut, altered and mangled, in a manner usual in the nineteenth century, to show off the talents and personality of star performers who commonly did not even trouble to rehearse with the supporting actors. One such star greatly admired by Shaw was Barry Sullivan, a tragic actor whose style was typical of the period: exaggeratedly passionate, heroic and rhetorical, such a style as was necessary to impress audiences in the large nineteenth-century theatres, where most people were a long way from the stage. When it was transferred to a smaller, more intimate theatre, the absence of subtlety in this style, and its remoteness from the manners and behaviour of everyday life, showed up. So it came to be ridiculed as 'ham' acting.

Indeed, since the eighteenth century, another form of entertainment had flourished which mocked at the heroic style. This was burlesque, which aimed to arouse more or less critical laughter in the spectators. Eighteenth-century burlesque, especially as written by Henry Fielding (1707–54), was sometimes an instrument of political satire, and this had led to the introduction of the system of censorship that continued to operate until after Shaw's death. In fact, there was very little actual censoring of plays on political grounds in all this time. Instead, it was almost universally accepted throughout the nineteenth century that the stage was not a proper medium for serious comment on politics, religion, or sex. The arrival of Ibsen's plays challenged this state of affairs.

Some of the visits Shaw made to theatres in London during his early years in the city are recorded in passages of his novels. Then, following his time as a music critic, he was appointed to be drama critic for *The Saturday Review*. The three-volume collection of the pieces he wrote for this paper, published under the title of *Our Theatres in the Nineties,* is a most valuable guide to what the London theatre was like in the last decade of the century. Certainly his experience of it sickened him of the most fashionable sort of play: the 'well-made play', translated or imitated from French originals, combining shallow feeling and superficial cleverness, treating rather sensational subjects in a mechanical and basically conventional manner.

Play writing: the first phase

The first of Shaw's plays to be performed, *Widowers' Houses* (1892), was written (on the basis of an earlier, abandoned attempt) in response to the need of the Independent Theatre for suitable material to present after *Ghosts*. In this and *Mrs Warren's Profession*, written soon afterwards, Shaw dealt with serious topics of a kind discussed by the Fabians, and employed a dramatic form and general style owing much to Ibsen's social plays. It was soon evident that he would have even more difficulty getting these publicly performed than he had had in trying to get his novels published. So he altered his style and wrote further plays along the lines of burlesque (as in *Arms and The Man*) or romantic melodrama (as in *The Devil's Disciple*), but twisting the conventions so as to express his serious and unconventional themes. Theatrical managements remained uninterested, so Shaw collected the dramatic works he had written and had them published by Grant Richards under the titles, *Plays Pleasant and Unpleasant* and *Three Plays for Puritans*. For this purpose he added to the text lengthy and often amusing descriptions of settings and characters, thus making the plays easier and more attractive to readers. This time the device succeeded, and the texts were enjoyed in the study before they received a fair trial on stage.

Marriage

Shaw had found time in his busy life for a long series of flirtations with interesting and able women, including the actress, Florence Farr, and Annie Besant, the social reformer who was to become the leader of the Theosophical Movement and, ultimately, a President of the Indian National Congress. He conducted a particularly charming flirtation entirely by letter with the most celebrated English actress of the age, Ellen Terry. Then in 1898 he married a wealthy upper-class Irishwoman and fellow Fabian Socialist, Charlotte Payne Townshend. It was a celibate marriage for companionship and it turned out very happily. Henceforth Shaw's domestic existence provided a stable, peaceful and orderly background to his career as a writer. He no longer needed to work as a journalist and, in addition to having his plays printed, he was able to lay out money for theatrical presentation of them to a general public. (But he engaged in a further, most famous flirtation with Mrs Patrick Campbell before she played Eliza in *Pygmalion*.)

Towards a National Theatre

From the time of his association with the Independent Theatre group, Shaw had remained in touch with the pioneers who wanted to break the stranglehold of commerce on the British theatre. Nearly all the fashionable theatres in the West End of London were controlled by men who looked on them as money-making businesses and had very little interest in drama. The result of this was that low standards of acting and production were common, and plays were chosen on the basis of what had drawn large audiences in the past; and audiences used to nothing better had become poor judges of quality. The remedy was seen to lie in getting, first, wealthy individuals and, ultimately, the Government to subsidise theatrical enterprises that aimed at artistic excellence. In 1894 Florence Farr put on Shaw's *Arms and the Man* in a short season at the Avenue Theatre, London, financed by Miss Annie Horniman who later endowed an Irish National Theatre. The Stage Society, the most important of the play-producing societies, working for the cause of a new, better quality drama, was founded in 1899 and gave a few private performances of several Shaw plays. At about this time Shaw's friend, William Archer, was working with a young actor, Granville Barker, towards the publication of *A Scheme and Estimates for a National Theatre* and, in 1904, Granville Barker took the Court Theatre to give a demonstration of what such a theatre could offer. The greater part of the money for this undertaking came from Charlotte and Bernard Shaw. The experiment was a triumphant success. Barker trained a fine company of actors and directed them with great skill. Shaw himself came in to help in directing his own plays, eleven of which were presented at the Court Theatre within the next three years. At the end of this time he was generally recognised as the leading dramatist of his day and the most considerable British dramatist since the eighteenth century.

The battle for an English national theatre was not won until the end of the second world war, when the setting up of the Arts Council ensured subsidies from public funds to theatre companies all over the country which were concerned with quality and originality in their productions. Shaw continued to advocate a national theatre until the end of his life, but the fate of his own plays was no longer so dependent on the breaking of the commercial monopoly. It had been established that Shaw's drama was entertaining and that audiences were eager to see it. So two well-known actor-managers, (Sir) Herbert Beerbohm

Tree and Mrs Patrick Campbell, relying on the combination of their reputations and Shaw's, put on *Pygmalion* in 1914. It was extremely popular and made a lot of money for all concerned.

The First World War and after

The conditions of the war which broke out later in 1914 seemed to undo all the efforts of the theatre reformers. Most of the younger men volunteered for the Army, or were conscripted into it. Granville Barker was one who never went back to his old profession. All that anyone now seemed to want of the theatre was the provision of bright and cheerful entertainment for soldiers home on leave; nothing which made people think, or even raised perplexing questions, had any chance of presentation in London's West End. Shaw himself was considerably over the age for joining the Army; but the general war hysteria, the destructive futility of the entire conflict, and particular stupidities of its conduct by politicians and military commanders, outraged his clear-sighted, rational approach to life. (Perhaps his Irish origins helped to keep him detached, too.) He published his criticisms as an 80-page supplement to *The New Statesman* under the title of 'Common Sense about the War' (1914). As a result, he was regarded as a sort of traitor by many people who had not read what he actually wrote. The play that he was starting in 1914 when the war began, *Heartbreak House*, was not produced until 1920, and the work he went on to, *Back to Methuselah*, is evidence of how his expectation of stage production receded. For, as he wrote, this work turned increasingly into a series of lengthy philosophical discussions in dialogue, paying slight attention to the practicalities of actual performance.

Shaw won his public back with *Saint Joan* in 1924. By this time he was in alliance with (Sir) Barry Jackson, a wealthy theatre enthusiast who established and financed a theatre in Birmingham along the lines laid down previously by Granville Barker. For the rest of his life, Shaw could count on Barry Jackson to give a showing of the new plays he wrote; and in 1929 Jackson set up an annual festival at Malvern, a country town in the West Midlands, devoted to the presentation of plays by Shaw and the music of Sir Edward Elgar. (After some years when the only Shaw festival in the world was held in Canada, at Niagara-on-the-Lake, the Malvern Festival was revived in 1977.) From 1912 onwards, Shaw generally arranged for the very first performance of each of his new plays to be given outside England. This helped to spread his fame and ensured that, when each work was seen in England, foreign critics had already established its reputation. For he continued to believe that English critics were biased against him.

He visited Moscow and had an audience with Stalin in 1931. In view of his own political commitment, it was natural that he should be sympathetic towards the problems of the USSR and ready to recognise its achievements. He was always tempted to take the opposite side to majority opinion on any matter, and there was a great deal of antagonism towards Russia in the England of that time. He championed Mussolini and even defended Hitler as examples of efficiency which the lazy and blundering English might profitably study. So he brought upon himself the charge of admiring dictators, hardly dispersed by his caricatures of them in one of his last considerable plays, *Geneva* (1938).

Charlotte Shaw died in 1943, to her husband's great grief. He lived on in the house at Ayot St Lawrence where they had received many visitors from all over the world. (Among these had been T.E. Lawrence (1888–1935), 'Lawrence of Arabia', whose admiration for the older man led to his using the name, Shaw, when he wanted to conceal his identity, during his service in the Royal Air Force.) Bernard Shaw continued writing almost until his death at the age of ninety-four, in 1950.

On principle, he had always refused public honours: titles, honorary degrees and even the highly exclusive Order of Merit. However, he did accept the Nobel Prize for Literature in 1926, giving his prize money for the publication of translations of Swedish drama into English. His own work has been translated into very many languages. A number of his plays have been turned into films, and Shaw himself co-operated in the filming of some, including *Pygmalion*. The fortune he had amassed was swelled after his death by royalties from the musical show and film, *My Fair Lady*, based on this same play. He had wished to leave his money for the establishment of a new alphabet, but realised that there might be little support for this. In fact, the other beneficiaries he named in his will have profited most: three public institutions, the British Museum, the Royal Academy of Dramatic Art, and the National Gallery of Ireland.

Shaw's beliefs

Before leaving Ireland, Bernard Shaw had already rejected Protestant Christianity for Free Thought. His mocking disbelief in supernatural forces led him to accept Naturalism, a favourite philosophy among literary men of the late nineteenth century in Europe and America. He expressed his point of view in the Preface to his collection of *Plays Pleasant* (1898):

> To me the tragedy and comedy of life lie in the consequences . . . of our persistent attempts to found our institutions on the ideals suggested to our imaginations by our half-satisfied passions, instead of on a genuinely scientific natural history.

Despite his enthusiasm for the scientific attitude, Shaw was unhappy about accepting the fatalism that might be inferred from Darwin's account of the evolution of species through natural selection; and, as a socialist, he was especially unhappy with the development of Social Darwinism, which fastened on the notion of the survival of the fittest to justify unbridled free competition and the worst excesses of capitalism. He found a way out through the doctrine of creative evolution as developed by Samuel Butler. This emphasised the importance of a non-individual will, such as appears in the philosophies of Schopenhauer and Nietzsche, in bringing about biological adaptation and development. *Back to Methuselah* with its attendant Preface (1921) presents Shaw's fullest statement of this idea. In his plays, he usually associates this intuitive, non-conscious will with women characters, for example: Ann Whitefield in *Man and Superman*, the heroine of *Major Barbara*, and Joan of Arc—whom he describes as possessing 'vital genius', a term related to the concept of *élan vital* developed by the philosopher Henri Bergson (1859–1941), the spirit of life itself. *The Adventures of the Black Girl in Her Search for God*, which Shaw wrote while travelling in Africa in 1932, shows all religions, all human ideas about the nature of God, as gropings after truth which reflect the degree of ignorance and savagery to be found in the believers. God, he suggests, is the end towards which human life may move, as it is attracted towards something greater than itself. Though he described himself, in his later life, as a deeply religious man, the articles of Shaw's faith are expressions of the values he held rather than abstract dogmas. After the first world war he found it harder to be optimistic about the future, but he continued to insist that mankind must accept self-responsibility.

The plays

All Shaw's plays are comedies, employing laughter as their medium for critical attacks on various kinds of error or foolishness. They all provoke thought as well as offering pleasurable entertainment. But they are certainly not all written to one formula: some are tightly constructed, while others are sprawling and unpredictable; the settings are sometimes contemporary, sometimes historical, sometimes fantastic; and Shaw's character-drawing varies from realistic to allegorical. The extent and nature of the laughter they arouse are equally variable. Shaw was widely read, and a great many influences from his reading were assimilated into his work, alongside the influence of the forms of theatrical entertainment he enjoyed in his youth. He claimed descent from the great classic authors of comedy, notably the Greek dramatist Aristophanes (c450–375BC) and France's greatest dramatist, Molière (1622–73), and from the Elizabethan dramatist, Ben Jonson; he also confessed a large debt to the nineteenth-century novelist, Charles Dickens. Among younger dramatists, Granville Barker successfully imitated some of Shaw's techniques in his own very different plays; but

Shaw's truest follower was the leading German playwright of this century, Bertolt Brecht (1898–1956), especially in his later plays.

A note on the text

Shaw wrote *Pygmalion* in 1912. It was first performed in German in Vienna in 1913, and the German translation was published in the same year. The English text first appeared in two magazines, *Everybody's* (New York) and *Nash's Magazine*, in 1914.

Though the play was first performed in England at His Majesty's Theatre, London, in April 1914, the text was not published there until 1916, when it appeared in a single volume together with *Androcles and the Lion* and *Overruled*, published by Constable. It was issued on its own in 1918 by the same publisher, with a title page describing it as: 'a Play in Five Acts: by a Fellow of the Royal Society of Literature'. (The ending used in the performance was changed in the printed text, and the specially written Afterword was added.)

Shaw made some alterations and wrote additional material for Gabriel Pascal's film of *Pygmalion*, first shown in October 1938, and later editions of *Pygmalion* were based on a selective version of the film script with a revised text of the Afterword. Penguin Books (New York and Harmondsworth, England) first published this in paperback form in 1941, with the description 'A Romance in Five Acts' on the title-page, and with illustrative drawings by Feliks Topolski; it has been reprinted many times since.

The dramatist himself supervised the printing of Constable's limited Collected Edition (1930–2) and Standard Edition (1931–50) of his plays and also the one-volume *Complete Plays* first published by Odhams Press, London, 1931, 1934–8, 1950, taken over in the final enlarged form and re-issued by Paul Hamlyn, London, 1965. The screen version of *Pygmalion* was substituted for the stage version in the Standard Edition and *Complete Plays* after 1940. The screen version without the drawings is included in *The Bodley Head Bernard Shaw: Collected Plays with their Prefaces*, IV, edited by Dan H. Laurence, Max Reinhardt, The Bodley Head, London, 1972. (This is the authorised edition which has replaced the Constable Standard Edition.)

Shaw's American publishers issued an edition of *Pygmalion* in: *The Theatre of Bernard Shaw. Ten Plays*, edited by Alan S. Downer, Dodd, Mead, New York and Toronto, 1961. Following the great success of the musical version of the play, *My Fair Lady*, Alan J. Lerner's adaptation of *Pygmalion*, with his lyrics for Frederick Loewe's music, was published by Max Reinhardt, Constable, in 1958, and then by Penguin Books in 1959.

The present notes take account of both the original stage play and the film text of *Pygmalion* with its additions and variations, which is now the most easily available form of the work. They do not take account of the Alan J. Lerner adaptation.

Shaw's typography

Shaw dealt directly with the printer of his plays and insisted upon faithful reproduction of his own preferences in matters of punctuation and spelling. In particular, he objected to the ugly appearance of apostrophes in words like 'don't', 'haven't', 'I've', which might occur frequently in any passage of dialogue that attempted to reproduce colloquial speech. So, where there is no possibility of misunderstanding, such words appear without the apostrophe as 'dont', 'havent', 'Ive', etc. Examples of his personal spelling system are: the use of an older *e* instead of *o* in 'shew'; a preference for the American-style *–or*, rather than *–our*, in such words as 'honor', and a more extensive use of *–z–*, rather than *–s–*, than was usual in English texts of his day (for example in 'apologize'). When he intended any word to be spoken with special emphasis, he followed the continental European system of letter spacing (for example 'y o u') and italicised only single-letter words such as '*I*'. All the authorised editions of Shaw's plays have followed these practices, except that some later reprints of the Standard Edition use larger type instead of letter spacing for emphasis. Shaw occasionally used phonetic script to represent Cockney dialect in the text of *Pygmalion*.

The stage directions

It was Shaw's regular practice to leave blanks in his notebooks when writing the dialogue of his plays and to go back and fill these with descriptions of settings, characters, etc., before sending the text to the printer. All this material was printed in italic type, and it has become customary to refer to all the italicised passages in a Shaw play as 'stage directions'. The term is strictly applicable to a fairly small proportion of the whole. The rest was intended to make the play more easily readable by people who were used to reading novels, but not dramatic texts. Of course much or all of what Shaw supplied verbally in printed directions would be seen, or otherwise conveyed, in a stage performance.

You should look at your own copy of *Pygmalion* and see whether it gives the original stage text, or the film script, and you should also look at the dialogue for examples of some of the following colloquial contractions: 'don't', 'haven't', 'ain't', 'weren't', 'what's', 'that's', 'let's'. Does your text keep to Shaw's peculiar system of typography?

Part 2

Summaries
of PYGMALION

A general summary

A poor flower-seller from the slums of London hears a conversation between two linguistic scholars (phoneticians) in a crowd sheltering from a rain storm after the opera. One of them has demonstrated his skill in identifying local dialects and boasts of his ability to teach people of lower class origin to talk like ladies and gentlemen. The flower-girl, Eliza Doolittle, decides to use the excessively generous tip she is given to buy herself some lessons, and she turns up at Professor Higgins's house next day to make the necessary arrangements. Higgins is with Colonel Pickering, the friend he met the previous night, and the two bet on his chances of so transforming Eliza's speech in six months that she can pass for a duchess at an ambassador's garden party. Higgins and Pickering are both bachelors, and the housekeeper, Mrs Pearce, has misgivings about the irresponsible way in which they are proposing to amuse themselves without thinking out the consequences for Eliza. However, when Eliza's father, Alfred Doolittle, arrives to protest at the immorality of their abduction of his daughter, it soon becomes evident that he has no real objection, but merely wants to gain something for himself from the situation. They easily buy him off and he, who would naturally and legally have the main responsibility for Eliza, is happy to leave her in their hands. The transformation of Eliza starts with cleaning her up and dressing her nicely, this involving her first intro-duction to the way of life of the well-to-do middle and upper classes. Speech lessons follow, and she proves to be a quick, intelligent, hard-working pupil.

Higgins organises her first public test by having her attend his mother's 'At-Home'. Apart from Pickering and himself, the other visitors are a widow and her son and daughter of the name of Eynsford Hill. Mrs Eynsford Hill is a gentlewoman with very little money, thoroughly respectable but acutely aware that she can only barely keep up appearances and that her son and daughter have lacked the usual advantages of the upper class. The son, Freddy, falls in love with Eliza on seeing her beautifully dressed and now most attractive. The daughter, Clara, is dazzled, too, and accepts her as a young woman of high fashion. Mrs Eynsford Hill knows better, as does Mrs Higgins, for Eliza's conversation veers between ridiculously formal and stilted banalities, such as remarks about the weather, and beautifully pronounced expressions of low class ignorance and superstition. The clash between Eliza's new manner and her view of life teaches Higgins the lesson that he cannot create a lady without paying attention to her mind and soul. He still does not realise, as his mother does, that the consequences of training Eliza in ladylike habits and tastes may be disastrous for her.

He wins his bet with Colonel Pickering: at the end of the six months, the two of them take Eliza into high society (to a garden party, followed by a dinner party and a visit to the opera, in the original play; to an embassy ball in the screen version), where she is universally admired. (In the screen version, she is suspected to be a foreign princess whose English is perfect in a way that the English of native speakers never is.) Shaw does not indicate precisely how the change has been brought about. There is something miraculous about the transformation of the sham lady who went to visit Mrs Higgins into the real lady Eliza has now become. Higgins takes all the credit to himself, and even Pickering sees Eliza's triumph as a reflection of Higgins's professional skill. This angers Eliza, who sees that her own efforts are undervalued and that Higgins does not regard her as a human being with real feelings, but as something inert, a doll that it has amused him to pass off as a living woman. He seems scarcely aware of her presence. Provoked, she ceases to be the obedient pupil and rebelliously asserts her independence. By leaving the house in Wimpole Street, Eliza forces Higgins to realise how much he has come to rely on her. He traces her to his mother's apartment, where she has taken refuge, and tries to persuade her to come back.

At this juncture Eliza's father puts in another appearance. He, too, is transformed: outwardly, from poverty to prosperity; inwardly, from cheerfulness to misery. It is a change that parallels Eliza's, but in his case it is the result of a legacy from a deceased millionaire, obtained for him through some careless words written by Higgins. The practical solution to the problem of Eliza's future is thus easily found: her father can do the conventional thing and keep her in the comfort to which living in Wimpole Street has accustomed her. Eliza recognises that she has the alternative of marrying Freddy Eynsford Hill. Higgins wants her back but, being a confirmed bachelor, makes no offer of marriage to her. Eliza herself is determined that she will never again go back to being subservient to him. The play has a teasingly inconclusive end: Eliza goes off with Mrs Higgins to church to see Alfred Doolittle properly married as a respectable plutocrat should be. Higgins stays behind, obviously confident that Eliza will come back as before.

Note on the title of the play

The title, *Pygmalion*, refers to a character from ancient Greek legend. In the *Metamorphoses*, a famous collection of stories by the Latin author Ovid (43BC–AD17), Pygmalion is presented as a sculptor who scorns living women and makes a statue of ideal beauty. He falls in love with this, kisses it, addresses it in flattering speeches, brings gifts to it, then dresses its nakedness in robes and jewels. Finally he prays to the goddess of love to give him the statue for his wife. He returns home and finds that the statue has come to life. The goddess herself is present at the marriage. Shaw introduces a character called Pygmalion into the last part of his longest play, *Back to Methuselah*. There Pygmalion is a young scientist at work on the task of creating human beings in his laboratory, in a fable of the far distant future. His own creation turns on him and kills him. The main source for the Pygmalion episode in *Back to Methuselah* seems to be Goethe's (1749–1832) *Faust* (First part, 1808; second part 1832).

A great many theatre goers who have enjoyed Shaw's play have very little knowledge of the story of Pygmalion and no direct knowledge of *Faust*. Yet these people recognise a general similarity between the plot of Shaw's play and one of the best known stories in the world, that of Cinderella, a favourite with children and the basis of a very popular pantomime entertainment, still revived every Christmas in some British theatres. A number of references to *Cinderella* are made in these *Notes*, and a full account of the story and the parallels in *Pygmalion* is given on pp 54–5. If you do not know *Cinderella* you may find it helpful to read these pages now.

Detailed summaries

Preface

When Shaw came to publish his plays, he supplied them with prefaces to make the volumes easier to sell, as they offered buyers two items for the price of one, an essay as well as a play. The relation between Preface and play is variable: sometimes the Preface gives an account of the origins of the play; sometimes it is a quite independent essay on one of the themes occurring in the play. The connection between the two is more often oblique than direct, and it is certainly never safe to suppose that the Preface is a key to the play, telling in straightforward terms what that is about.

The Preface to *Pygmalion* is an aside to the play. It gives information about the actual phonetician Henry Sweet, whom Shaw used as a model for his character Henry Higgins. It is misleading in its statement that Shaw decided to have a phonetician for his hero because of the vital importance of making the English speak their language properly; and it is misleading in its later insistence that the play's 'subject is esteemed so dry' and that it is an 'intensely and deliberately didactic' work. Phonetics is not the subject of the play, but part of its plot-machinery; and the dramatist does not expound Higgins's phonetic system. In fact, Shaw is taking an indirect way to advertise his skill in interesting and pleasing audiences, whatever topic he chooses. He does not distinguish carefully between the descriptive science of phonetics and the teaching of elocution, the art of speaking well.

Differences between the original Preface and the revised version issued with the film script include: addition of a passage on Gregg shorthand and considerable changes in the final paragraph of the text; removal of references to Thersites and Ajax (characters from Homer), to the Academy of Dramatic Art and to Forbes Robertson (a well-known actor who played the lead in Shaw's *Caesar and Cleopatra* and *The Devil's Disciple*).

NOTES AND GLOSSARY

old foreign alphabet: the Latin alphabet; this reference introduced into the second version

in black and white: in print without ambiguity; in the second version only

Ibsen: Henrik Johan Ibsen (1828–1906), the Norwegian playwright and poet. See Introduction, pp. 7–9

Samuel Butler (1835–1902): opponent of Darwin's theory of natural selection, was also the author of a satire, *Erewhon* (1872), which influenced Shaw's *Back to Methuselah* (1921), and of a famous autobiographical novel, *The Way of All Flesh* (1903)

Satanic: arrogant as the angel who fell from heaven through pride

South Kensington: a district in West London

Joseph Chamberlain (1836–1914): a statesman and a leading figure in the Liberal Party at the height of its power, campaigned for his Imperialist ideas in 1903 and following years

Sybil: usually spelt 'sibyl', a prophetess. The name is of ancient Greek origin and there were various famous Sibyls in the ancient world

cloistered existence: kept in academic seclusion, rarely seen in public

two several times on two different occasions

set the Thames on fire: achieve something very remarkable

Poet Laureate:	holder of a Crown appointment granted to a leading poet; replaced, in the second version, by the name, Robert Bridges, Poet Laureate from 1913 to 1930. Bridges wrote a study of Milton's prosody. His most famous work was *The Testament of Beauty* published in 1929, the year before his death at the age of eighty-six
Ruy Blas:	a play by Victor Hugo (1802–85)
Theatre Français:	French National Theatre usually known as the Comédie Française
West End:	(fashionable area of London) . . . bi-lingual: (having learnt to imitate upper-class accents). This sentence is not in the original version of the Preface
honest and natural slum dialect:	Shaw removed 'and natural' in revising the Preface, as socially conditioned dialects are no more natural than slums
vulgar dialect of the golf club:	a snobbish way of speaking; replaced by 'the plutocracy', a term for the newly rich, in the revised Preface.

Act I: First Section

Mrs Eynsford Hill and Clara (as we later discover them to be) are waiting for Freddy to bring them a cab. They have come out of a theatre to find the rain pouring down, and they have taken shelter in the portico of St Paul's Church, Covent Garden. Freddy returns to say that all the cabs have been taken. They send him off once more but, as he goes, he bumps into a young flower seller (Eliza). Mrs Eynsford Hill is suspicious, when she hears this creature address her son as Freddy, and attempts to find out how she knows him by paying her sixpence. Eliza simply points out that she used 'Freddy' by chance as a typical name for a young man-about-town. The group sheltering in the portico is joined by Colonel Pickering. When he gives the flower-girl three-halfpence, all the loose change he has, a bystander draws attention to another man who is taking notes of whatever Eliza says. The girl's alarm is increased when people in the crowd accuse this man of being a police informer, though a closer look at him reveals that he belongs to the upper classes and his notes turn out to be written in phonetic symbols. The general hostility to this man (Higgins) turns into wonder and amusement as he demonstrates his skill in identifying speakers' places of origin from their pronunciation; but Eliza remains uneasy. The rain stops; Mrs Eynsford Hill and Clara go to catch an omnibus, and the rest move off in various directions leaving Eliza, Pickering and Higgins alone.

NOTES AND GLOSSARY

St Paul's Church: the film script adds: '*not Wren's cathedral but Inigo Jones's church in Covent Garden vegetable market*', referring to Sir Christopher Wren (1632–1723), greatest of English architects, and Inigo Jones (1573–1652), famous designer and architect. This church, which has been restored, is a masterpiece of simplicity and proportion. The Covent Garden area also holds the Royal Opera House and the Theatre Royal, Drury Lane. The fashionable members of the sheltering group are likely to have come from one or other of these theatres. The famous market itself has recently ceased to operate

close to the one on her left: note how precise some of Shaw's directions are, even placing characters on stage as if he were actually producing the play

cab: a term used at this time for both horse-drawn carriages and motor cars for hire on the streets

He wont get no cab ... missus: the double negative and the form of address are used by Shaw as features of lower-class speech (middle-class and upper-class speakers would only use 'Mrs' directly followed by a name). It is a literary convention to indicate the vulgarism by using the spelling 'missus'

Theatre fares: passengers who have been to a theatre

it aint: colloquial equivalent of 'it is not'; 'it isn't' would be usual today

gumption: spirit of enterprise, practicality; colloquial term

Charing Cross—Ludgate Circus—Trafalgar Square—Hammersmith: all actual London localities, Hammersmith much further west than the others, which are all within moderate walking distance of Covent Garden

Strandwards: towards the Strand, which leads into Trafalgar Square

orchestrates the incident: the word 'orchestrate' is an indication of Shaw's deliberate artfulness in using theatrical effects to suggest that Freddy's collision with Eliza (the Flower Girl) is in some way momentous

Nah than ... deah: 'Now then, Freddy: look where you are going, dear'. The flower girl speaks Cockney, the London dialect associated only with the lower classes by this time

Theres menners ... the mad: Cockney for 'There's manners for you! Two bunches of violets trodden into the mud'

shoddy: made of poor quality material

pray: a rather out-of-date equivalent of 'if you please', suggesting that Mrs Eynsford Hill (the Mother) is a rather old-fashioned and formal person

Ow, eez ... f'them: 'Oh, he's your son, is he? Well, if you'd done your duty by him as a mother should, he'd know better than to spoil a poor girl's flowers and then run away without paying. Will you pay me for them?'

a tanner: slang term for a coin worth sixpence that is no longer part of the British currency

Do hold your tongue: be silent. This expression seems very impolite today, as it did not when *Pygmalion* was written

a sovereign: a gold coin later replaced by the paper one-pound note

Garn!: 'Go on!' or 'Get along with you!' Slang expression of disbelief, used coaxingly here

tuppence ... hapence: Shaw's spellings correspond to the normal pronunciation of 'twopence' and 'half-pence'.

bloke: man; slang term recently revived

blessed: used colloquially as a very mild swear-word

I aint done nothing: another example of the grammatically incorrect double negative combined with the colloquial 'aint' (isn't)

a respectable girl: not a member of the criminal underworld

so help me: shortened form of 'so help me God.' Eliza is prepared to swear on oath that she has done nothing wrong

A tec: a detective; colloquial abbreviation

dunno: don't know, carelessly pronounced

Theyll take away my character ... on the streets: Eliza fears that those in authority ('They' is vague), probably represented by the police, will find her guilty of offensive behaviour towards Pickering and will not allow her to go on selling flowers; this would drive her to prostitution, the very offence of which she was unjustly suspected

aw rawt: all right

e's a genleman: he's a gentleman

bə-oots: distorted pronunciation of 'boots'

a copper's nark: slang term for a police spy

what youve wrote: this grammatical form is a sign of lower class speech

agen me: against me

molestation: a legal term for the offence of pestering someone

Course: of course

Nice thing: used sarcastically

blooming: used as a mild expletive like 'blessed' above, but more typically Cockney

Selsey: a small town on the south coast of England

Lisson Grove: in the Edgware Road district of London

four-and-six a week: a considerable rent for a comfortless bed-sitting-room in Edwardian England

Park Lane, for instance: the Bystander seems to be a Socialist. Only the very wealthy could afford to live in Park Lane in the West End of London

Housing Question: a contemporary political issue

Hoxton: an industrial district associated with political agitation

Bly me!: this vulgar exclamation is usually spelt 'Blimey!'

Aint no call . . . he aint: he has no cause . . . he hasn't.

what never, who never: not standard grammatical usage

have no truck with: idiomatic expression meaning 'have nothing to do with'

taking liberties: idiomatic expression meaning 'interfering', 'pushing (oneself) forward'

Cheltenham, Harrow, Cambridge, and India: the course of an upper-class education: through a preparatory school in the socially select, or snobbish, town of Cheltenham; then to the great public school at Harrow; so to Cambridge University; and finally a spell of service as an Army officer administering what was then the British Empire in India

Told him proper: low-class use of the adjective instead of the adverb 'properly'

toff: Edwardian slang term for a well-dressed person, a gentleman

where he come from: 'come' seems to be a survival of the subjunctive in local use

Earlscourt: usually Earls Court, a very respectable, but not first-class address

Epsom: in Surrey, a pleasant area outside London, where wealthy people interested in horses and horse-racing had their homes and maintained stables

knowed: knew

copper: slang for policeman, now largely replaced by Americanisms

Anwell: failure to pronounce an initial h- was the commonest of vulgar speech habits. There was a lunatic asylum in Hanwell

So long: colloquial expression of farewell

Act I. Second Section

The Note Taker (Higgins) explains to the military Gentleman (Pickering) that he is a professional phonetician and that his study is profitable to him on account of the newly rich, or self-made, men who will pay him for lessons in speaking standard English. He boasts that he could teach the flower girl so successfully that, in three months, she could pass for a duchess, or get a job serving the middle and upper classes.

It turns out that the other gentleman is also a student of languages and that the two of them are familiar with each other's work and have been eager to meet. They go off together, but not before Eliza has had a chance to hear where Higgins lives. She tries again to sell her flowers to them before they leave and is rewarded with a handful of money from Higgins, who apparently wants to make up to her for the insulting things he has said of her. Thrilled to discover how much she has been given, she takes the cab Freddy has eventually found and goes off in style to her lodgings.

NOTES AND GLOSSARY

worrited: a nineteenth-century colloquial variant of 'worried' rarely heard today

The science of speech: an inexact definition, as phonetics is concerned only with sounds

brogue: now applied only to Irish accents

Quite a fat one: this use of 'fat' is restricted to combination with such terms as 'living', or 'cheque', or 'sum (of money)'. It has connotations of comfort, luxury

They want to drop Kentish Town: upper-class speech is not necessary for making money, but is necessary for social acceptance among the middle and upper classes. Kentish Town is in the East End, the poorer part of London

place of worship: the first indication of the setting included in the dialogue. The Flower Girl's retort is a reminder that the Church of England professes to make no distinction between rich and poor. The Note Taker then carries on the line of association by speaking of her 'soul', 'the divine gift of ... speech' and referring to the Bible

tickled: amused

Whats that you say?: Eliza has been quick to catch the hint of what would be, for her, a very good job. Her silence during the following passage of dialogue suggests that she is listening for more

you squashed cabbage leaf: this vituperative description might have been suggested by the sight of refuse from the vegetable market

27A Wimpole Street: an address very suitable for a professional consultant

The Carlton: probably the exclusive gentlemen's club near St James's Palace. Its members are Conservative in politics

a jaw: slang for a good, unrestricted talk; old-fashioned now

Pharisaic: self-righteous, a common term of biblical origin. Higgins has, in effect, been preaching to Eliza

a half-crown: a coin worth two-shillings-and-sixpence, no longer in use

florins: two-shilling pieces; the word is rarely heard today

Damnation! Freddy swears in the Flower Girl's presence, a point to be remembered later

no object to me, Charlie: an additional passage is inserted in the film script at this point: Eliza orders the taxi driver to take her to Buckingham Palace, in order to impress Freddy, and only later does she give him her home address

make her hop it: Eliza's high spirits are expressed in her comically racy direction to the driver. This line is not in the film script

Judy: a conventional name for a woman of the people, counterpart to Freddy for a fashionable young man; only in the film script

For the film, Shaw wrote a continuation at this point, presenting Eliza's arrival in Angel Court, giving a brief passage of dialogue between her and the cabman, who admires her spirit, then describing the poverty of her room and the mood of excitement and hope on which she goes to bed.

Impidence: impudence

alarum clock: sleeping late could be disastrous to poor workers who might lose their jobs as a result. But the presence of the clock is also a further link in addition to the many original details that the story of Eliza shares with the widely known legend of Cinderella (who is threatened with finding her magic ball dress changing back into rags, if she stays at the palace after the clock has struck). See pp. 54–56 below on the Cinderella story.

Act II: First Section

In Wimpole Street, the next morning, when Higgins has just finished showing his equipment and explaining his researches to Pickering, the housekeeper, Mrs Pearce, announces the arrival of a young woman. This is Eliza, specially dressed for the occasion, and come to propose taking lessons from Higgins so that she may be able to get work as a lady in a shop. Higgins's first impulse—to get rid of her quickly—is checked when he realises how serious she is and what a considerable sum, by her standards, she is prepared to pay. Pickering, similarly impressed, confirms Higgins's interest and determination by challenging him to prove that he can transform her into a great lady. They bet on it, and Higgins is eager to start at once. He drops his openly bullying manner to Eliza and, instead, starts coaxing her with exaggerated fantasies of the life in store for her if she agrees. Mrs Pearce's sensible warnings are swept aside by Higgins's enthusiasm. Eliza, overwhelmed and alarmed, is given into the housekeeper's charge and sent away to be thoroughly cleaned up.

NOTES AND GLOSSARY

Higgins's laboratory: by calling it this, Shaw emphasises the fact that the Professor conducts his experiment here, and through his science manufactures a lady

a dessert dish . . . chocolates: Higgins is a self-indulgent man

No paintings: there is very little colour in this room. Colour is associated with emotion, and it is a room devoted to intellectual pursuits

Bell's Visible Speech: Shaw's Preface refers to the inventor of this system of phonetic signs, Alexander Melville Bell

Broad Romic: a kind of phonetic script devised by Henry Sweet

lingo: slang for 'language'

saucy: rarely heard today in the sense of 'impertinent'

what I come for: 'what I have come for'

yə-oo/tə-oo: despite his earlier statement that he would not continue to reflect Eliza's pronunciation in his spelling, Shaw could not resist noting this version of 'you' and 'too'

baggage: slang term for 'woman'

at bay: Shaw employs the metaphor of the hunted animal

stead: carelessly spoken form of 'instead'

sellin: the pronunciation of -ing as -in could be heard among fashionable people as well as the poor when the play was written (as in 'huntin', shootin', and fishin'')

at the corner of Tottenham Court Road: Eliza seems to have moved a little south of her usual station, on the previous night. There would be more chance of custom near the theatres at that hour

genteel: like the language of ladies' maids and shop girls, very carefully polite and correct, rather than natural

zif: as if

Youd a drop in: this particular idiom (meaning 'You'd drunk a good deal') is at least as familiar in Irish speech as in Cockney. The stress falls on 'in'

'Eliza ... three in it': the point of the rhyme Higgins begins and Pickering continues is that all the other names are familiar or affectionate versions of Elizabeth: so there is one girl, not four, involved. This nursery rhyme joke helps keep the play close to the imaginative world of nursery days and fairy tales.

Hold your tongue: this is peremptory, but not quite as rude as it later seemed

with a broomstick: this object is frequently mentioned in folk tales and often associated with magic. In not speaking simply of a 'broom' or 'brush' Higgins works on Eliza's imagination of Mrs Pearce as a frightening witch-like creature

you was: a common lower class solecism for 'you were'

Whats this for?: Eliza has started to learn about being a lady

It's no use talking ... that way, at all: Mrs Pearce's intermediate social position and her greater attention to other people make her more aware of the ways of the poor than Higgins is. She sees that Eliza is bewildered by Higgins's jocular and teasingly indirect manner of speech (as in 'thats your handkerchief ... one for the other'). Presumably Eliza just sniffs, though she might occasionally wipe her face with the back of her hand

give me that handkerchief ... her property: Eliza has very little property she can call her own, and Higgins is about to order the destruction of her clothes while talking of Eliza herself as somebody's property. The handkerchief seems to have special value to her as a gift from Higgins, as his ring has later

real good: really good

so deliciously low: note how colourfully exaggerative a style Higgins likes to use; compare 'draggle-tailed guttersnipe', which follows

Monkey Brand: the trade name of a harsh detergent, commonly used for scouring cooking pans. Note Doolittle's later comparison of Eliza to a monkey

Whiteley: Whiteley's was one of the great Edwardian department stores, or 'emporiums' as they labelled themselves

talk of such things: Eliza has grown up thinking that the naked human body is something to be ashamed of

wallop her: beat her; the verb has a comic ring to it

the streets will be strewn: such is the effect of the heroine's beauty in Max Beerbohm's well-known fantasy *Zuleika Dobson* (1911)

off his chump, off his head: slang for 'mad', 'crazy'

balmies: lunatics; from the slang adjective usually spelt 'barmy'

take you ... and dress you beautifully: this goes beyond Higgins's original undertaking; Shaw is moving closer to the Cinderella story

Her that turned: she who turned

She'll only drink if you give her money: Higgins glibly produces a late Victorian objection to distributing money to the lower classes

I got: instead of 'I have' prompts Higgins's recognition that he has to teach Eliza to speak grammatically

Ive heard of girls being drugged: Eliza is thinking in terms of the seduction of innocents, a public scandal in late nineteenth-century London

have ate it: have eaten it

you shall marry: Higgins now starts to spin a fairy story to Eliza. Fairy stories, often more sophisticated versions of folk tales, usually play down the frightening aspect of magic and stress its power to fulfil the heart's desires

She's incapable ... what we are doing: note the way Higgins twists about in his reasoning. Giving two different excuses throws doubt on the genuineness of each, but the second is more interesting than the first

As a military man ... enough for her: to suit his purposes, Higgins assumes Pickering to be the kind of officer he obviously is not, and he argues from a false analogy

walloped by Mrs Pearce with a broomstick: Higgins is casting his housekeeper in the role of a witch to frighten Eliza into doing what he wants

I always been: I have always been

I never offered to say a word to him: It is not absolutely clear whether Eliza means 'I never contradicted him', or whether she is still protesting that her behaviour outside St Paul's Church was innocent

plaints are no longer audible: the film script follows this with scenes in a spare bedroom and adjoining bathroom, showing the cleaning up of Eliza

the likes of me: common Cockney for 'people like me'

copper: a vessel made of copper for boiling laundry

catch my death: shortened form of 'catch my death of cold'

He's made of iron: Eliza's opinion of Higgins is that he is inhuman, not just physically strong. Note this reversal of the idea of Pygmalion and the statue

I dursnt: an older form of 'I dare not'

reely: this represents the vulgar pronunciation of 'really'

I never done: I have never done

Act II: Second Section

Higgins explains to Pickering why he is a bachelor and also that he has a professional code of honour as a teacher which guarantees Eliza's safety with him. Mrs Pearce, the housekeeper, warns Higgins of the need to set Eliza a good example by not swearing and being tidier and cleaner in his personal habits than he usually is. Higgins's view of himself is belied by his handling of Alfred Doolittle, Eliza's father, who has called at Wimpole Street in the hope of making some profit for himself out of the gentleman's interest in Eliza. Doolittle, who arrives dressed in the working garb of a dustman, is a strongly individualistic personality who speaks eloquently on behalf of the social type he represents, which the middle class condemns as 'undeserving'. But, formidable as Doolittle may seem, Higgins is more than a match for him, using various forms of threat and intimidation, together with a five pound note, to ensure that Doolittle will not trouble them again. As the dustman is about to leave, Eliza appears transformed into a lovely girl hardly recognisable to the others as the shabby flower seller they knew. She points out that a luxurious bathroom is not available to poor women, but her puritanical sense of shame over nakedness and sex emerges again. Doolittle now does actually leave, making it plain that he is handing control over Eliza to Higgins, and recommending the use of a strap to keep her in order. Pickering's polite way of speaking to her is a contrast that Eliza appreciates. She shows signs of contempt for her old associates, and this prompts Higgins to warn her against snobbery. Her vanity is aroused, too, by the new clothes supplied for her to wear.

NOTES AND GLOSSARY

a man of good character: Pickering, of course, wants to be sure that Higgins will not exploit Eliza sexually. Higgins takes the question in a much wider sense

That thing!: Higgins is referring to the unattractive sight of dirty Eliza in her shabby clothes

seasoned: made resistant by long exposure. The term is usually applied to wood

Eliza's hat: Arthur Morrison's story, 'Lizerunt', in *Tales of Mean Streets* (1894), had illustrated the pride girls from the slums took in showy hats, imitating the very elaborate hats worn by fashionable ladies

put it in the oven: to sterilise it as Eliza's hair is infested with lice

particular: careful, selective

comes to anchor: as if he was a ship

benzine: a chemical used to clean fabrics

Youre: You're, you are; an instance of Shaw's avoidance of apostrophes in type-setting

Doolittle: the name is more appropriate to her father than to Eliza. Shaw's occasional use of names with an obvious meaning, corresponding to a leading trait in the particular character, is in the tradition of allegory and of the comedy of humours (temperaments) written by Shakespeare's contemporary, Ben Jonson. Shaw admired Jonson and regarded Bunyan, the seventeenth-century allegorist and writer of *The Pilgrim's Progress*, as one of England's greatest authors

blackguard (*pronounced* blagard): a generalised term of abuse without the upper-class associations of the otherwise roughly equivalent 'rotter'

If theres any trouble he shall have it with me: Higgins seems to have forgotten the view of himself he has just claimed in relation to Mrs Pearce

Governor: a common term of respect at this time, used by small boys to and of their fathers, as well as by social inferiors to those above them

magisterially: with the air of a judge

fairity: justice, fair play; an unusual word

You got: You've got

Where do I come in: What (profit) is in it for me

a brass farthing: a worthless coin; common expression

a poser: a question very difficult to answer

put her up to it: suggest it to her

native woodnotes wild: a phrase applied to Shakespeare's poetry by John Milton (1608–74) in his poem 'L'Allegro'

Welsh ... mendacity and dishonesty: for centuries, the English have accused the Welsh of lying and stealing as part of their national character. It was in the nineteenth century especially that the art of pulpit oratory was most cultivated in Wales. The political character and talents of David Lloyd George (1863–1945), who had become a prominent Liberal statesman at this time, caused a revival of jibes against the Welsh

you was: you were

corner of Long Acre and Endell Street: quite close to Covent Garden. Street corners are favourite sites for public houses

The poor man's club: public houses where the poor spent money on drinking alcohol were regarded as much less respectable than the decorous gentlemen's clubs which usually prided themselves on having a good wine cellar.

afore: before; rather archaic

to oblige you like: to oblige you, as it were

worse than death: Higgins uses a conventional phrase associated with sensational literature and melodrama. No sophisticated Englishman or woman of this time would be likely to regard chastity as the greatest of female virtues, though most still regarded it as a virtue

Heres a career opening for her: Doolittle may still believe that Higgins has procured Eliza for prostitution

monkey: street musicians often carried monkeys around on their shoulders. Evolutionary theory was commonly thought of as proving that men were descended from monkeys

men of the world: sophisticates whose free-ranging talk might easily embarrass simpler people

sell your daughter for £50: in 1889, a very well-known journalist, W.T. Stead, had shocked the late Victorian public conscience by an account (under the heading of 'The Maiden Tribute of Modern Babylon') of the large numbers of poor girls in London who were forced into prostitution. In the course of gathering his evidence, Stead had himself bought a young girl who was under the legal age of consent. Eliza's insistence on her respectability, and the whole scene between Doolittle and Higgins, needs to be seen in the context of the public outcry Stead had aroused

undeserving poor: the character of Alfred Doolittle is a personification of this social group. He has picked up the phrase from late Victorian public discussions of how the poor could best be helped, and he uses it as though it was a neutral description of a class, not implying moral condemnation (as, of course, it does). The prevalent late Victorian morality of hard work, careful spending, and saving as much as possible, essentially a capitalist morality, is totally opposed by Doolittle

needs is: needs are

hearty than him: heartily than he

cause: because

I aint: I am not

growed: grown

has any ginger in it: has any spice, or kick, in it, Shaw ironically portrays Doolittle as caring about the *quality* of life, as any moralist should

It wont pauperize me: it won't ruin my character by turning me into a beggar. 'Pauperize' is a word invented in the course of the disputes about helping the poor by doling out money and goods to them without requiring services in return. Some feared that the effect of this was a demoralisation of character, breaking down pride, self-respect, and the spirit of independence and initiative. A debate on the subject is presented in Chapter Fifteen of E.M. Forster's novel, *Howards End* (1910)

spree: spell of fun and enjoyment, with plenty to drink; nineteenth-century slang

the missus: common vulgarism for 'my wife'

throwed: thrown

why dont you marry that missus: Pickering has jumped to the conclusion that Doolittle is not married to Eliza's 'sixth stepmother'

catch her marrrying me!: shortened form of 'You won't catch her . . . The woman in question understands that legally married women are possessions in their husbands' power

and dont know no better: and doesn't know any better

she's only a woman . . . happy anyhow: Doolittle subscribes to the view, very convenient for him, that the female personality is naturally masochistic

his booty: usually loot stolen in battle

cunningly: skilfully, with artistry

By Jove!: upper-class exclamation which substitutes the name of a Roman deity for 'God'

why ladies is: why ladies are. Since *Pygmalion* was written, an increasing tendency for 'lady' to be associated with uselessness and snobbery has resulted in a growing preference for the general word 'woman'. Granville Barker (1877–1946), Shaw's close friend and theatrical associate, wrote a definition of the lady in his play, *The Madras House*, in 1910. This runs: 'an epitome of all that aesthetic culture can do for a woman ... the result ... of three of four generations of cumulative refinement ... Creatures, dainty in mind and body, gentle in thought and word, charming, delicate, sensitive, graceful, chaste, credulous of all good, shaming the world's ugliness and strife by the very ease and delightsomeness of their existence; fastidious—fastidious—fastidious; also in these latter years with their attractions more generally salted by the addition of learning and humour. Is not the perfect lady perhaps the most wonderful achievement of civilisation, and worth the toil and the helotage of—all the others?'

a lick of the strap: the right of married men to thrash their wives and children without interference from the police or anyone else has only quite recently been denied under the law

free-and-easy ways: Eliza understands these words as a reference to upper-class immorality, to which nakedness is likely to lead, in her view

the plate: the collection plate taken round at church services

your lip: your cheek, your over-ready answers

a mug: a fool; slang. Doolittle ignores Higgins's sarcastic reference to his 'blessing' and concentrates on the thought of the advice he might give Eliza

so long: colloquial for 'goodbye'

mam: 'maam' in film script, usually represented as 'ma'am', a form of 'madam' used respectfully to a superior

collecting dust: Eliza may be making a joke, punning on the word 'dust' which could be used as a slang term for 'money' in the nineteenth century, when 'dustman' could be used as the equivalent of 'money grubber', as well as having the standard meaning of 'collector of garbage'. Dust also refers to the material from which human beings are made, which needs the addition of a soul to give it life. Shaw's favourite novelist, Charles Dickens, had taken the great dust heaps of contemporary London as the central symbol of his late novel, *Our Mutual Friend* (1864–5). Boffin, the character who comes into a fortune based on the recovery of valuable objects from the refuse, is described by Dickens as 'the golden dustman'. Some aspects of Doolittle's personality recall another character from the same novel, Silas Wegg, who gets money out of Boffin and then goes searching for further profit among the dust.

Theyve took it out of me: they've taken it out of me, they have tormented me

The film script adds a brief scene in which Higgins and Pickering give Eliza a formal lesson in pronunciation. She is a very quick, intelligent pupil, but the learning process is a painful ordeal for her.

Act III

Higgins visits his mother when she is officially at-home to friends. She asks him to leave because his bad manners offend her guests; but he tells her that Eliza will be among the callers and explains the nature of the task he has undertaken and the problems that remain. While he is talking, Mrs and Miss Eynsford Hill are announced. Colonel Pickering is the next to arrive, followed by Freddy Eynsford Hill. While waiting for Eliza, Higgins makes tactless conversation and, in particular, comments on the dangerousness of speaking one's thoughts honestly in society. Eliza enters, looking so beautiful that everyone is impressed and Freddy falls in love with her on the spot. It is now that Higgins recognises the Eynsford Hill family as people who were present when he first met Eliza. His pupil follows his instructions to talk only about the weather and people's health (the usual small talk of English polite conversation), but her manner of doing so is not at all what he had in mind, and it bewilders the Eynsford Hills. The climax comes when Eliza rises to go and utters the swear word that Mrs Pearce, in Act I, had warned Higgins to stop using in Eliza's hearing. Clara accepts Higgins's mischievous explanation that Eliza's way of speaking is the latest fashion, and she is prepared to imitate it herself. When Mrs Higgins is left alone with her son and Colonel Pickering, she tries to make them realise how irresponsible they are in playing their game with Eliza without considering what is to become of her afterwards. She compares the girl's probable future with the plight of Mrs Eynsford Hill as a poor gentlewoman; but the two men brush her anxieties aside.

NOTES AND GLOSSARY

Chelsea Embankment: a favourite London address for artists because of the beauty of its views over the River Thames

Morris: William Morris (1834–96), artist and designer of interior decorations, writer and socialist, challenged the values of nineteenth-century industrial society and pioneered the modern revival of craftsmanship. Morris wrote a poetic version of the Pygmalion legend and included it in his long poem, *The Earthly Paradise*

Burne Jones: Sir Edward Burne Jones (1833–98), a very successful Victorian painter in a romantic and mannered style. He was closely associated with Morris and produced designs for tapestries and stained glass windows

ottoman: a circular padded sofa with a centrally placed backrest most often seen today in museums and art galleries for the use of visitors. The word is of Turkish origin

Whistler: James McNeill Whistler (1834–1903), an artist of American origin who lived for many years in London and painted some famous views of the Thames in a very individual style of impressionism that shocked conservative art-lovers

Cecil Lawson: Lawson (1851–82) was a landscape painter who exhibited a number of pictures of Cheyne Walk and the Thames.

Rubens: Shaw may be thinking particularly of the paintings which the great Flemish artist Peter Paul Rubens (1577–1640) supplied for the Luxembourg Palace

Rossettian: in the style of Dante Gabriel Rossetti (1828–82), leader of the Pre-Raphaelite Brotherhood, a group of painters and poets (including Burne Jones and, for a time, Morris) who sought inspiration from medieval sources. The graceful and colourful romantic costumes in Rossetti's pictures had considerable influence on late-Victorian fashion

Chippendale: Thomas Chippendale (1718–78), a famous eighteenth-century cabinet-maker, who gave his name to a style of furniture

small talk: trivial polite conversation

some habits lie too deep to be changed: Shaw is consistent in presenting Higgins (his Pygmalion figure) as the type of man who does not marry. He makes the point psychologically convincing by this insistence on Higgins's devotion to his mother

Ahdedo?: how do you do? Shaw is hinting that upper-class pronunciation can distort the English language as much as Cockney does

the Royal Society: the British national academy for the advancement of science, founded in the seventeenth century

what they really think . . .: the notion that civilisation depends on hypocrisy occurs frequently in Shaw's writings

the dickens: a mild oath

it wouldnt be decent: this anticipates Eliza's sensational offence against decency at the climax of this Act

the H in Higgins: failure to pronounce an initial aspirate was about the commonest sign of vulgar speech

The shallow depression . . . barometrical situation: Eliza's technically-worded speech is in the wrong linguistic register for conversation; she has been reading meteorological reports in newspapers. The rest of her conversation, with its beautifully pronounced vulgarisms of style and content, is all the more comic for its contrast with this first pronouncement

Killing!: Slang. An equivalent of 'terrific', or 'terrifically funny'

I hope it wont turn cold: the whole of this speech from Mrs Eynsford Hill illustrates the sort of remark that Higgins had intended Eliza to make

Lord love you!: vulgarism, used for emphasis

She come: she came

gin: a popular alcholic drink among the poor, and among poor women in particular

What become: What became

pinched it: stole it; slang

them as: those who

done her in: did her in; explained in the text

Them she live with: those she lived with

Something chronic: colloquial understatement for 'very heavily'

what I could see: that I could see

regular: vulgar use of adjective in place of adverb

he had a drop in: variant of colloquialism 'he had a drop taken', meaning he had drunk a good deal of alcohol

lots of women has: lots of women have

booze: alcohol; slang word

proper: right, properly

what was you: what were you

Not bloody likely: Shaw's choice of expression here was very precisely calculated and got one of the longest laughs recorded in the theatre, throughout the first run of *Pygmalion* in London. He had chosen a word everyone knew, but which was taboo (forbidden by custom and inhibition) in middle-class polite usage; it could not be uttered by ladies, or by men in the presence of ladies. The fact that newspapers reporting on the play avoided printing 'bloody', but used instead such euphemisms as 'the sanguinary epithet', testifies to the sense of its impropriety in respectable public contexts. It was an excellent example of language marking an arbitrary, irrational, yet very strong distinction between social classes and, even more, between the male and female sexes. For 'bloody' is an essentially meaningless word, a simple intensifier. (Its derivation from the medieval religious oath, 'By our Lady', would have been unknown to all except students of etymology.) The fact that Shaw's audiences responded with laughter, not horror, indicates that the taboo on the word had weakened a little by 1914, but not enough to destroy the shock-value of its pronunciation in the theatre. Beerbohm Tree (1853–1917), the actor-manager who played Higgins, tried to persuade Mrs Patrick Campbell (1869–1940) not to speak the word, as he was nervous about its reception; but the actress knew that Shaw had given her the opportunity for a tremendously effective exit

Theres no right or wrong in it: Clara is quite correct in seeing that there is nothing criminal or sinful about the use of expletives and slang. However, she is too simple-minded to realise how codes of manners and standards of speech maintain a system of social inequalities

Pitch it in strong: Do it thoroughly; a figurative expression

She goes out radiant . . . silvery laughter: her own breaking of the taboo, with Higgins's encouragement, has an immediate positive effect on Clara. There is a touch of sound psychology in this, as release from any inhibition shows in a freer flow of vitality

reeking with the latest slang: Mrs Eynsford Hill's 'reeking' is a figurative usage moving very close to slang

Hyde Park: London's largest open space

perfectly cracked about her: even Mrs Higgins has been infected by the freer atmosphere following Eliza's breaking of the taboo, and uses a slang expression meaning 'infatuated with her'

her soul: Higgins has discovered that Eliza is a complete person, not just a talking object. Some critics have read this passage carelessly and accused the Professor of trying to alter her soul

your live doll: it is unlikely that Shaw could have used this phrase in his play without remembering Ibsen's (1828–1906) *A Doll's House* (1879) whose heroine discovers the need to become an adult person in her own right, not just a doll for a man, father or husband, to play with. Mrs Higgins regards the tendency to treat women as live dolls as a sign of immaturity in men

speaking together: a sign of their excitement. Shaw referred on several occasions to his skill in arranging dialogue for voices as though he were composing musical duets, trios, quartets, or ensemble pieces

Lehár: Franz Lehár (1870–1948), a Hungarian composer of light operas, of which the most famous was *The Merry Widow* (1905)

Lionel Monckton: a very successful English composer (died 1924) of musical comedies, generally produced at the Gaiety Theatre, London

A problem: problem plays, as they were called, had a considerable intellectual following in the 1870s to 90s. Among the principal authors of this type of drama were the French writers, Augier and Dumas *fils*

Ripping: a slang expression of enthusiasm

The film script has an additional passage of narrative leading up to a scene in dialogue which represents the Embassy reception where Eliza finally passes for a princess. The expense of presenting such a scene on the stage may have been a factor in Shaw's decision not to include it in his original stage play. The climax of the fairy story of Cinderella is the ball at the royal palace, where the poor girl appears dressed as a princess; but Shaw was not simply re-telling the Cinderella story and was undoubtedly more interested in what would happen after Higgins had won his bet. However, film presentation demanded a ball scene. In supplying one, Shaw brings in another character: a former pupil of Higgins's, a Hungarian, who is a master of many languages. By this means the author is able to inject a little dramatic tension into the scene, as it seems that Nepommuck's expert knowledge may lead him to suspect the truth about Eliza. But, on the contrary, it is he who spreads the rumour that she is a (Hungarian) princess. Gabriel Pascal producer of the film of *Pygmalion*, was a Hungarian, and Shaw may have been joking at his part, as an imitator of Pygmalion in bringing Eliza to life on the cinema screen.

Pandour: a fierce type of private guard or soldier

little Nepommuck, the marvellous boy: Shaw must have had a good reason for substituting this name and character for 'Professor Nepean', the rival of Higgins whom Eliza refers to, in the original stage version. Some suggestions can be made here, but there is no way of knowing certainly whether any, or all, account accurately for Shaw's choice: (*a*) Nepom(m)u(c)k is a place name associated with the patron saint of Bohemia, about whom there was a tradition that his tongue was perfectly preserved when the rest of his body decayed; (*b*) 'n'ap'o'muck' (=not a ha'penny of muck) is a possible dialect expression meaning 'without any money'; (*c*) it may not be entirely a coincidence that Thomas Mann (1875–1955) in his novel, *Doktor Faustus* (1947), gives the same name and description to the young nephew of his modern Faust, Adrian Leverkühn. Shaw and the German writer may have drawn on the same (unidentified) source. Mann associates his Nepomuk (the more usual spelling) with Ariel and Echo from Part II of *Faust*, the masterpiece on which Goethe worked at intervals for the greater part of his life, and with Euphorion, the legendary child of a marriage between Faust and a materialisation of the spirit of Helen of Troy, whom Goethe presents as a symbol of ideal beauty. Instead of vanishing, as Euphorion does, Shaw's Nepommuck has grown up into something very different from the image suggested by 'marvellous boy'. It seems possible that Shaw wished to hint that Higgins's laboratory could be thought of as a place where artificial human beings had been created, as if by magic arts, before the Professor set to work on Eliza

Mrs Langtry: Lily Langtry was an actress who became the mistress of King Edward VII

An ordinary girl out of the gutter: Higgins obviously shares the belief Shaw stated on other occasions: that hypocrisy is so general in society, no one believes the truth when it is spoken

---

Act IV

Eliza, Higgins and Pickering return to Wimpole Street after their evening in high society (after a garden party and a dinner party, in the original version). The two men talk to each other about the day, as though Eliza was not in the room. Higgins expresses relief that the whole experiment is over, and Pickering congratulates him on his triumph. They go off to bed, Higgins giving Eliza his orders for the morning, just as if she were his servant. When he returns for the slippers he has forgotten, Eliza is so angry that she throws them at him. This leads to a scene between them, in which Eliza voices her feelings and her present view of the whole affair. Higgins shows his arrogance and insensitivity, his absorption in himself and his own affairs. Eliza succeeds in upsetting him by asking in the most scrupulous way just what belongs to her, and preparing to give the rest back, as though she is about to leave. He goes out of the room at last, in a fit of bad temper. Eliza looks for the ring he gave her, which she has flung down. The original version of Act IV ended at this point, with the implication that Eliza still values her relationship with Higgins. In revising the text for the Collected Edition of his plays, Shaw added two sentences of directions to Eliza which show his anxiety to avoid finishing the scene in a sentimental way: Eliza, even angrier than Higgins, is to throw the ring down again, after she has found it.

NOTES AND GLOSSARY

La Fanciulla del Golden West: an opera (known in English as *The Girl of the Golden West*) which was still new, having had its first performance in 1910. It is by Giacomo Puccini (1858–1924)

my slippers: the incident with the slippers calls to mind a commonly criticised domestic ideal: of the comforting wife who brings her husband's slippers when he arrives home after a hard day's work. But it is probable that Shaw was also following out his parallel with the Cinderella story, in which slippers—glass ones worn by Cinderella at the ball—lead eventually to the happy ending: her marriage to the Prince

coroneted billet-doux: the letter which looks like a love letter and has a coronet on the envelope is an example of false appearances that corresponds in a sharply ironic way to Eliza in her fine robes and jewels

flings herself furiously on the floor, raging: Shaw's plays include many instances of strong emotion displayed in such a physical manner

where you picked me out of: an inelegant, not strictly correct phrase. Shaw is careful to show that the transformation of Eliza is not too perfect to be credible.

What am I fit for? Eliza herself puts the question that was troubling Mrs Higgins in Act III. It is a key question in the play as a whole and applies generally to any lady, not simply to Eliza

feel so cheap: feel off-colour, or slightly unwell; slang expression now rarely heard. Shaw may have chosen the words carefully because their other possible meaning, 'feel worth so little', is particularly apt to Eliza's present condition

I didnt sell myself: the analogy between marriage and prostitution was frequently drawn by contemporary feminists

Tosh: nonsense; Edwardian slang term

togs: clothes; slang term

the millenium: here means simply 'heaven on earth'

shied: threw; a colloquial word

experiment: Eliza appears to link the word with scientific experiments on animals. Shaw had used the notion of vivisection (experimentation on live animals) as an image of callous treatment of human beings in his early play, *The Philanderer* (1893).

The film script proceeds to a scene in Eliza's room, where she changes into ordinary clothes before leaving the house. Just outside, she encounters Freddy who has been gazing up at the windows in the hope of glimpsing her. He declares his love for her and she gratefully responds. They are moved on by police constables on two occasions, before a taxi comes by. They decide to ride in it all night, and Eliza states her plan of calling on Mrs Higgins in the morning to ask her advice.

a crawling taxi: Shaw was evidently using the taxi as a recurrent motif in *Pygmalion*. Its counterpart in the Cinderella story is the magic coach

Wimbledon Common: a piece of surviving countryside just south of London

Act V

Higgins and Pickering call on Mrs Higgins, next morning, with the news that Eliza has disappeared from Wimpole Street. They have called on the police to help find her and they are justifying this action to Mrs Higgins, when the maid announces the arrival of a gentleman called Doolittle. This turns out to be Eliza's father transformed by expensive clothes, but complaining about his bad luck. He accuses Higgins of ruining his life by carelessly recommending him to an American millionaire. This man has recently died and left Doolittle a considerable annual income. The new wealth has taken him out of his old social class and turned him into a member of the middle class with a new sense of responsibility. As a result, his happy and carefree approach to life has given way to melancholy. Mrs Higgins is pleased to think that Doolittle will be able to support his daughter, but Higgins is unwilling to give her back to her father. Mrs Higgins reveals that Eliza is upstairs and makes clear to her son and Pickering Eliza's reasons for running away. She asks Doolittle to go out on the balcony, then asks Eliza to come down. The girl begins by treating Higgins and Pickering with conventionally pleasant politeness, as if they were just slight acquaintances. She goes on to talk to Pickering as if Higgins wasn't there, and she criticises the latter's whole manner of treating her. But her composure breaks down completely for a moment, when she catches sight of her father. He tells her that he has not only come into money, but that he is also on his way to his wedding; for Eliza's 'sixth stepmother' has reacted to their new prosperity by wanting to be respectable in the middle-class manner. The others agree to go along to see him married. Eliza is left alone with Higgins for a while, and they start arguing in a way that is almost a courtship on Higgins's part, while Eliza defends her claim to respect as an equal and independent human being. The two now seem equally matched in strength, and neither is prepared to give in and admit defeat; at the same time, their liking for each other and basic good humour are apparent. Mrs Higgins reappears and takes a still defiant Eliza off to church, leaving Higgins to mock at the idea of her marrying Freddy.

NOTES AND GLOSSARY

tell Miss Doolittle: in the original stage version, this is the first indication that Eliza has gone to Mrs Higgins. It is evident that Shaw does not want to keep the audience in suspense over her whereabouts; he wants to focus on other, more important matters

confounded: a mild expletive

bolted: run away (like a runaway horse)

ass of an inspector: stupid inspector

very particular: very particularly

Genteel relatives! now we shall hear something: Higgins is anticipating the kind of revelation often made towards the end of popular novels or in the last act of plays in which the main interest lies in the story

Doolittle enters: Shaw had employed the device of introducing a character in Act I and bringing him back transformed, in the last act, in his first play to be produced, *Widowers' Houses* (1892). He seems to be following a dramatic formula used by Ibsen in *Rosmersholm* (1886), where Ulrik Brendel, a broken-down intellectual looking like a tramp, appears unexpectedly in Act I and again unexpectedly in the last act, when his outward appearance is somewhat improved but his optimism has changed to bitterness. What Ibsen says of 'the Rosmer way of life', that 'it ennobles, but it kills joy', corresponds to Doolittle's view of middle-class morality

You done: You have done

What the dickens: Whatever; 'dickens' is a common substitute for 'devil' in an expletive used for emphasis

Enry Iggins: Doolittle drops the initial aspirates with pride and dignity

Ruined me: a paradoxical statement here, as the expression usually implies the loss of money, bankruptcy, when it is used by a man

two conversations with you: Doolittle's visit in Act I was evidently not his last and only attempt to get money out of Higgins. This is an example of how a dramatist can suggest that his characters are real people who go on living outside his play

blighter: nuisance; slang term

that wanted you: who wanted you

give him the chance: gave him the chance

Americans is: Americans are

reckonise: The omission of the g in 'recognise' is commonly heard in lower class speech

Them words is: Those words are

a lark: an amusing incident; not often heard today

making a gentleman of me: as Higgins has made a lady of Eliza—by more laborious means

live for others and not for myself: Doolittle has had virtue forced upon him

by this: by this time

proper English: the proud dustman thinks of middle-class English as the deviant form

chuck it: throw it away, give it up

the nerve: the courage

intimidated: Doolittle implies that the whole social and economic system depends on keeping people afraid of poverty

acause: because

Excuse the expression: refers to the expletive 'blasted'

Skilly ... Char Bydis: garbled forms of Scylla and Charybdis in a proverbial saying that refers to a channel between two perils in Homer's *Odyssey*; Scylla originally a nymph, was changed into a sixheaded monster by Circe and was opposite the whirlpool of Charybdis in the straits of Messina, between Italy and Sicily

Broke: ruined, beggared; slang

jolly: frequently used as an intensifier in Edwardian English

fire-irons: poker, tongs and shovel usually kept by the hearth. Mrs Higgins's sense of her own worth is stronger than Eliza's

let bygones be bygones: forget the past

Pick: the shortened form allows Higgins to indulge in a pun on his friend's name and the verb 'picked'

I taught it to you: Higgins has not yet realised that learning makes the pupil independent of the teacher

take me in: deceive me

created ... out of the squashed cabbage leaves: recalls the detail that Cinderella's coach is made out of a vegetable (a pumpkin)

spraddling: sprawling; a dialect word today

St George's, Hanover Square: a favourite church for fashionable society weddings

that common low woman: Eliza's own rise in the social scale has not cured her of a wish to look down on others

turned off: Doolittle may have the two slang meanings of this phrase in mind: 'married' and 'hanged'

comes to words: quarrels

tremenjous: represents the vulgar pronunciation of 'tremendous'

brougham: a closed carriage

very cunning: very cleverly

sportsmen: implying that they have looked on the whole business as a game

nailed him: secured him (as a husband)

there was two: there were two

I been the victim: I have been the victim. Solidarity with his own sex overrides class solidarity or family ties as far as Doolittle is concerned

gets his back to the door: this preliminary physical dodging about is a foretaste of the mental dodging in which Higgins, even more than Eliza, is about to engage

passed over: ignored, neglected

turn the machine on: While the immediate reference is to the gramophone, this also suggests a robot, or artificial woman

twist the heart: Higgins's last speech has certainly been lover-like, but Eliza is alert to his capacity for unscrupulous emotional blackmail

a woman fetching a man's slippers is a disgusting sight: there is no evidence that Higgins has reflected on this before

because it was my job: Higgins was indignant when Eliza said substantially the same about him to Pickering: 'that is his profession'

I'm a slave now: Eliza's discovery about her new position is much the same as her father's

Than he is: by making this correction of her grammar Higgins is able to avoid commenting on the substance of what Eliza has said. He could be letting her down gently

sitting on his heels: a figurative expression here. Realisation that he can feel jealous of Freddy has knocked him back

I only want to be natural: in contrast to being made into something, an artificial or cultural process

give up feeling neglected: the whole of this part of the scene between Higgins and Eliza goes over the same ground as the scenes between Philip and Jessica Madras in Granville Barker's play, *The Madras House* (1910). While they were working closely together in the theatre, Shaw and Barker made constant and deliberate cross-references to each other's plays that would have been evident to regular patrons of the seasons Barker directed at the Court Theatre and elsewhere

I'll marry Freddy ... as soon as hes able to support me: the last clause was revised by Shaw to read more realistically: 'as soon as I am able to support him'. From this point there are a number of divergences between the original text and the film script. The more significant will be noted

assistant to Professor Nepean: in the original text; the film script substitutes 'that hairy Hungarian' (Nepomuk). It is clear from the context that Nepean is Higgins's professional rival; the choice of name may have been arbitrary and therefore liable to be changed when Shaw thought of a better

by the way, Eliza: Higgins is confident that he has won in the struggle and got Eliza where he wants her, in spite of the words she has just spoken to him

Buy them yourself: in place of this sharp retort from Eliza, in the original version, the film script gives her a longer speech ('Number eights are too small for you . . . What you are to do without me I cannot imagine') which implies that she still accepts responsibility for looking after Higgins

I'll buy you the tie and gloves: Mrs Higgins's promise is found only in the stage version, where its effect is promptly cancelled out by words from Higgins ('She'll buy em all right enough')

buy em: buy them

she's going to marry Freddy . . . Ha ha ha ha ha !!!!!: in the film script only, where the laugh makes an enigmatic end to the work

They kiss . . . highly self-satisfied manner: in the original version. It seems significant that it is his mother, not Eliza, that Higgins kisses; but the following description of his behaviour still makes a teasing ending to the play

Narrative Afterword

The play is, of course, complete without this, and is to be judged apart from it. Shaw seems to have written the Afterword to check criticism of his ending to the play. He argues that a marriage between Eliza and Higgins would be unsuitable and unlikely, in view of the nature of the two characters. Then he turns his attention to establishing, as fact, Eliza's marriage to Freddy. He tells the story of their financial difficulties and ultimate success with a flower shop, and of their continuing relationship with Higgins and Pickering. Incidentally, he indicates how Alfred Doolittle is taken up by the aristocracy and how Clara Eynsford Hill changes gradually but radically after learning the truth about Eliza. The account ends with a more precise explanation of Eliza's continuing attitude to Higgins.

The reader who has been satisfied by the play may well grow impatient with the Afterword and feel that Shaw is himself infatuated with the characters he treats in this way, out of their dramatic context. Indeed there seems to be an autobiographical element in his description of Higgins here; and a reading of the correspondence between Shaw and Mrs Patrick Campbell can lead to the conclusion that the Afterword presents a view of the dramatist's relationship with the actress (who married George Cornwallis West as Eliza is supposed to marry Freddy) under the guise of Higgins's relationship with Eliza. Although there are many interesting and amusing comments in the Afterword, the piece as a whole seems to lead the attention away from the play.

NOTES AND GLOSSARY

romance: the word is ambiguous. Besides the definition reflected in Shaw's comment on the improbability of Eliza's transformation, it can denote a love story

a disentanglement which persons of genius achieve ... by parental fascination: Shaw may well have written this whole paragraph out of his own personal experience

Landor's remark: Walter Savage Landor (1775–1864) was an English man of letters

her Pygmalion: the Afterword makes explicit the link between Eliza's story and the Greek legend as the text of the play never does

Nietzsche: the quotation comes from *Thus Spake Zarathustra*. The famous German philosopher was among the principal influences on Shaw's thought, but we need not suppose that this particular precept is seriously recommended

his Nietzschean transcendence of good and evil: this probably alludes to Doolittle's remark that he 'like the rest of us' is partly an honest man and partly a rogue, though it could also apply to his understanding of the relativity of class morality

quarter herself on Wimpole Street: take up living quarters in Wimpole Street

Mr H.G. Wells: Wells (1866–1946), the novelist and social reformer, was for a short time a leading member of the Fabian Society along with Shaw

a girl of her own age who dazzled her: this is Eliza

General Booth: William Booth (1829–1912), founder and leader of the Salvation Army

Gypsy Smith: Rodney Smith (1860–1947), a famous evangelist of gipsy parentage; closely associated with William Booth and later with the Young Men's Christian Association

Galsworthy: John Galsworthy (1867–1933), English novelist and dramatist. His best-known work is *The Forsyte Saga*, a portrayal of the upper-middle class in English society. It began with *Man of Property* (1906); sequels were published in 1918, 1920, and 1921

blackening the Largelady scutcheon: dishonouring the Eynsford Hill family

Porson or Bentley: Richard Porson (1759–1808) and Richard Bentley (1662–1742), famous English scholars of ancient Greek literature, especially concerned with textual study

classy: high class

swank: swagger, showing-off

mulish: stubborn

Galatea never does quite like Pygmalion: no name is given to the statue made by Pygmalion in the ancient sources. A quite different Greek story of a sea nymph called Galatea is the basis of the opera *Acis and Galatea* (1721) by George Frederick Handel (1685–1709). W.S. Gilbert (1836–1911) wrote a dramatic burlesque *Pygmalion and Galatea* (1871). It is likely that Goethe's *Faust*, Part Two, where Galatea appears as a figure of ideal beauty, was influential in the transference of the name into the Pygmalion legend

Part 3

Commentary

The general nature of the play

Realism and fantasy

Pygmalion is set in London near the beginning of the twentieth century. Shaw's descriptions of the scene for each act imply that he wanted a realistic representation, first of the area close to St Paul's Church in Covent Garden, and then of rooms such as might be found in the houses of the upper-middle class. By giving directions for a taxicab to be driven on to the stage in Act I, he seems to be carrying the principle of realism rather far. In fact, the unusualness of this in a play is striking and likely to cause amusement rather than making the stage seem more like an actual street. (When the play was made into a film, the taxicab in the street was a conventional sight on the screen, and Shaw had to bring it back later to make sure that the audience would notice it particularly.)

The realistic settings give support to Shaw's presentation of his characters as real people who might well have been living in London when he was writing. He introduces the main characters in Act I, as members of a crowd, and associates them with various districts likely to be familiar to the audience watching the play in a London theatre. The cumulative effect of naming so many actual localities is to create an illusion that the events of the play take place in the actual world in which we live. But we are not altogether deceived. A number of highly improbable things happen in the course of the play, and Shaw has recognised this fact by describing *Pygmalion* on the title page as 'A Romance'. It is easier in some societies than others for a person of humble origins to make his or her way into a higher social class. Eliza Doolittle's original notion of what she might achieve is fairly modest: from selling flowers in the streets she might graduate to employment in a florist's shop. Higgins's skill as a teacher would have been demonstrated adequately if it had helped her to become a shop-assistant in a West End store. Instead, she is mistaken for a duchess, or a princess, at the end of a quite brief process of education, most of which is supposed to have taken place in the intervals between acts of the play. Thus Shaw has sacrificed realism to make the drama more exciting and amusing. When he adds to the transformation of Eliza an even more surprising, because less prepared, change in her father, it is quite evident that this play is not consistently representing life as it is. It comes nearer to day-dream and wish-fulfilment than to observation and experience. Indeed the contrast between Eliza in Act I and Eliza in her ball gown, and between Doolittle in his dustman's clothes and in his wedding finery, could be described as magical.

Coincidences sometimes happen in real life, but in a novel or play they very easily suggest that the author is arranging incidents as he wants them. Shaw makes use of coincidence at several points in his play:

(a) Pickering meets the scholar he has come to England to find, in the crowd at Covent Garden where Eliza can overhear them;

(b) the guests who meet Eliza at Mrs Higgins's flat were also in this crowd;

(c) Doolittle comes into a fortune at the same time as his daughter achieves her great success in society.

The second of these coincidences does not seem particularly necessary to the plot of the play; and the effect of the third is exaggerated by the suddenness with which Shaw reveals the change in Doolittle. It is evident that the dramatist is drawing attention to the fact that this is not life but art and under his control. We are invited to enjoy the way he organises events and the patterns he designs. We can be confident that the characters' fates are in his hands and that he will dispose of them as he thinks fit; they are not struggling unaided against society, nature, time and chance.

Comedy and seriousness

One effect of bringing an element of fantasy into the play, and keeping us conscious that this *is* a play, is to make our approach to the whole less solemn and serious. We can relax in response to signs that Shaw is offering us entertainment and that he means us to enjoy ourselves. Day dreaming is usually a lazy business and can leave us in an almost drugged state. To counteract this Shaw brings in another form of entertainment that is a great energiser: he makes us laugh. The main source of comedy in the play is the character of Professor Higgins, and he is comic:

(a) because of the contrast between his view of himself and the way he appears to others, including the audience;

    (*b*) because he is a clown in social situations, bumping into furniture, failing to observe polite manners and, on occasions, being outrageously tactless;

    (*c*) because he is determined to get his own way and we can see him manipulating and deceiving others to this end, with a mixture of the innocent selfishness of a baby and the wiliness of a rogue;

    (*d*) because he is full of verve, energy, high spirits which are infectious and make us euphoric, too.

He enters on the business of teaching Eliza as a game, and this light-hearted, essentially irresponsible spirit colours the play. Doolittle provokes laughter by turning upside down accepted opinions and ways of thinking, introducing confusion in place of a clear-cut distinction between what is reasonable and nonsense. In addition, there are many incidental jokes scattered throughout the play, as when Eliza reverts to her Cockney exclamation of surprise at seeing her father:

LIZA ... I have learnt my lesson. I dont believe I could utter one of the old sounds if I tried. (*Doolittle touches her on her left shoulder. She drops her work, losing her self-possession utterly at the spectacle of her father's splendor*) A-a-a-a-a-ah-ow-ooh!

It is commonly felt that works which offer amusement and entertainment are inferior to those which approach obviously important themes in an earnest manner, present unpleasant truths, communicate sadness or pessimism, and perhaps demand considerable effort of concentration from audience or readers. Yet Shaw breaks down the distinction between amusement and enlightenment, jest and earnest. (Higgins, the character, pursues his work with tireless enthusiasm, for the fun of it, and reflects the dramatist's own outlook in so doing.) *Pygmalion* is a thoughtful play which challenges commonly-held beliefs and prompts a reconsideration of some of the central assumptions on which British society has been based.

An incidental example of this is Doolittle's presentation of himself, in Act II, as 'one of the undeserving poor':

Think of what that means to a man. It means that he's up agen middle class morality all the time.

This is amusing in its unexpectedness: instead of describing himself as a victim of poverty, Doolittle complains that he is a victim of morality. He backs up this claim by pointing out that middle class people (or the government) undertake to help the needy but, in fact, are only prepared to give rewards for what they consider moral behaviour:

If theres anything going, and I put in for a bit of it, it's always the same story: 'Youre undeserving; so you cant have it'.

He reflects on the fact that receiving money that has not been earned is not always regarded as wrong:

> my needs is as great as the most deserving widow's that ever got money out of six different charities in one week for the death of the same husband.

Then he argues that the things he wants money for are not vicious but necessary to the physical and spiritual well-being of the human nature all men share (though moral men, according to middle-class orthodoxy, curb and suppress that nature):

> I dont need less than a deserving man: I need more. I dont eat less hearty than him; and I drink a lot more. I want a bit of amusement, cause I'm a thinking man. I want cheerfulness and a song and a band when I feel low.

When Higgins proposes to give him a five pound note, Pickering comments: 'He'll make a bad use of it, I'm afraid'. These words imply that the dustman will squander the money on drink; but Doolittle challenges Pickering's moral judgment (middle-class morality again) by referring to the virtues and benefits of such squandering:

> one good spree for myself and the missus, giving pleasure to ourselves and employment to others, and satisfaction to you to think it's not been throwed away. You couldnt spend it better.

He refuses an additional five pound note on the grounds that it is too much for such a spree, and he shows a firm grasp of the idea that those for whom the future is uncertain tend to make the most of life in the present, whereas a degree of financial security leads to anxiety about the future. In fact, Doolittle's remarks reveal another consistent morality, contrary to that accepted by the middle class. The opposition can be expressed in these terms:

The values of capitalism	The values of the underprivileged
work	idleness
thrift	open-handedness
respectability	high spirits
abstinence	festive eating and drinking
prudence	happiness
responsibility	freedom from care
puritanism (self-denial)	hedonism (pleasure-seeking)

We soon gather that Doolittle also approves a form of serial polygamy in opposition to the middle-class ideal of strict and chaste monogamy;

and his current 'missus' enjoys more independence and respect from him than if they were legally married.

This analysis, though tedious compared with Shaw's dramatic method, serves the purpose of showing how much serious matter is implied in the passage, and how it leads the mind towards the conclusion that all morality is relative to some particular condition of life. In Shaw's presentation, Doolittle is not tedious but entertainingly comic. If there was no serious content in what he says, we should quickly find him silly and stop laughing. As it is, the realisation that there is a good deal of matter for thought packed into his words intensifies our sense of the comedy, which in turn prevents us from separating out the ideas from our amusement.

The story

Pygmalion and Cinderella

Shaw has invented the specific story of Eliza and Higgins, but it is a variant on one of the best known basic, or archetypal, stories in the world. He has not needed to mention this openly for its presence to be recognised whenever the play has been performed. As the story of Cinderella it is told to children in their nursery days, and has been the favourite story for treatment in Christmas pantomime. The devisers of pantomimes had taken it over from the nineteenth-century extravaganza tradition which, in turn, had borrowed it from Perrault's elegant eighteenth-century French version of a very widespread and ancient folk tale. The same basic narrative pattern is found in a number of other traditional European stories, including the tales of Griselda (retold by Chaucer (1340–1400) in *The Canterbury Tales*) and of King Cophetua and the beggar maid. It is easy to understand the reason for the story's popularity: it tells how a humble, despised and ill-treated girl had her goodness and beauty recognised and rewarded by being made a great lady, loved and married by a prince or king; as such, it satisfies the longings of the neglected among women and men's dreams of the power to be gracious, magnanimous and protective; it affirms the supreme value of goodness and implies that it may be perceived and rewarded by a supernatural power.

The essentials of the Cinderella story in its pantomime and nursery forms are:

(*a*) the heroine is motherless, and her father is impoverished, weak, and neglectful of her;

(*b*) she is the youngest of three sisters, the two elder being ugly and cruel;

(c) at the centre of the story is the grand ball given by the Prince, to which the Ugly Sisters go, leaving Cinderella in the kitchen, wishing that she could be there, too;

(d) her fairy godmother appears and, by her magic, conjures up a beautiful dress and a splendid coach for Cinderella to go to the ball, but warns her that she is to leave at the stroke of midnight, or her finery will turn back to rags;

(e) Cinderella is greatly admired as some unknown princess;

(f) the Prince dances with her and falls in love with her; she stays till the clock is striking twelve and then, in running away, loses one of her glass slippers;

(g) the prince succeeds in finding her again when the glass slipper, which has been tried on all the other girls around, proves to fit her perfectly;

(h) the fairy godmother arrives again and dresses Cinderella fitly for her marriage to the prince;

(i) the family's other servant, a clown called Buttons in the pantomime, is Cinderella's loyal friend throughout;

(j) the prince also has a friend and confidant, a courtier named Dandini.

Listing these particulars makes it easier to see what Shaw has included in *Pygmalion* and what alterations he has made.

He has simplified the plot by cutting out the Ugly Sisters, and he has made the story more realistic by omitting the Fairy Godmother and her magic and the business of leaving the ball at midnight. He has also left out the finding of Cinderella through the glass slipper, and her subsequent marriage to the Prince. Yet he seems to have been at pains to keep a connection with the fairy tale, for a closer look reveals that some of the apparent omissions are to be found in the play in another form or displaced, in another context. The most obvious instance is the magic coach, replaced by the taxi which Eliza sees as the grandest mode of transport. The striking clock is heard in Act I; the slippers remain important, though they now belong to Higgins and are not made of glass. These are now Cinderella motifs, rather than essential elements in the story. Eliza, like Cinderella, runs away and is found again by Higgins, though this episode has been stripped of its fairytale quality. The play also ends with a wedding: Doolittle's, not Eliza's. Shaw seems to have introduced new elaborations by bringing the Eynsford Hill family into the story, but it is possible to see Mrs Eynsford Hill and Clara as replacing the Ugly Sisters, who also do not recognise the Cinderella they know when they see her in her fine clothes; and the omission of Buttons has made room for Freddy. The part played by the Fairy Godmother in transforming Cinderella is substantially taken over by Higgins with the assistance of Pickering (his Dandini, the confidant;

see (*j*) above, though Mrs Pearce does the initial cleaning up and dressing of the girl, and Mrs Higgins takes over as her female friend and protector. Thus:

(*a*) The ball is replaced by the garden party, or embassy reception;

(*b*) Cinderella's coach is replaced by the taxi;

(*c*) the Cinderella motifs of the striking clock and the slippers remain in *Pygmalion*;

(*d*) the marriage of Cinderella and the Prince is replaced by the marriage of Doolittle;

(*e*) the role of the Fairy Godmother in magically transforming Cinderella is taken over by Higgins, with the help of Pickering;

(*f*) the practical aspect of the Fairy Godmother's role in dressing Cinderella for the ball and generally acting as her friend and protector is shared between Mrs Pearce and Mrs Higgins;

(*g*) as Cinderella runs away and is found again by the Prince, so Eliza runs away and is found again by Higgins;

(*h*) Pickering is Dandini to Higgins's Prince;

(*i*) the Ugly Sisters are replaced by Mrs Eynsford Hill and Clara;

(*j*) Buttons, the clown, and Cinderella's loyal friend, is replaced by Freddy.

Shaw has achieved a double effect through this combination of altering and yet retaining details from the Cinderella story: he has created his own, new and individual story, more realistic than Cinderella; and he has given this new story a more universal quality and a more general appeal, all the stronger for its reminiscence of childhood half-beliefs in good magic and happy endings. The freedom with which he has altered and displaced details corresponds more closely to the folk processes which anthropologists have discovered in studies of multiple versions of particular myths than to the learned, literary process of simply modernising an ancient legend.

Shaw's use of the legend of Pygmalion

The alterations have also made possible the combining of Cinderella material with other mythic elements. Shaw's choice of title prompts recognition that he had another legend in mind while shaping the play. These are the main similarities and significant differences between the story of Pygmalion as told by Ovid and the story of Higgins and Eliza:

(*a*) Pygmalion is a sculptor;	Higgins is a student of linguistics, a kind of scientist;
(*b*) Pygmalion shuns women;	Higgins is a confirmed bachelor;

(c) Pygmalion makes a statue of an ideally beautiful woman;	Higgins trains Eliza to the point where she talks and behaves like a beautiful automaton;
(d) Pygmalion falls in love with his statue, pays court to it, showers it with gifts and dresses it in robes and jewels;	Higgins cajoles Eliza with deceitful promises, gives her chocolates, buys her clothes, gives her a ring and hires jewels for her to wear;
(e) the statue comes to life, in answer to Pygmalion's prayers to the goddess of love;	Eliza becomes a real lady and asserts her independence of her teacher;
(f) Pygmalion marries his ideal beauty.	Higgins evades marrying Eliza.

Again Shaw has avoided bringing the supernatural element of the original (the part played by the goddess) into his play. So the bringing of Eliza to life has to be figurative, not literal, and it is appropriate that Shaw's substitute for Pygmalion should be a teacher. Making him a teacher of speech determines that Eliza must be changed into an articulate young woman, able to use words fluently and well: the statue must be made to speak. As articulacy and intelligence are conventionally associated, it follows that her intelligence also should seem to come alive. Most importantly, Higgins's profession gives Shaw the opportunity of widening the implications of Eliza's story to bring in the theme of speech habits as marking class distinctions.

Other legends recalled in *Pygmalion*

By giving Higgins a laboratory Shaw has introduced a point of similarity with the character he calls Pygmalion in his later play, *Back to Methuselah*. There the sculptor of the classical legend is replaced by a scientist who creates human beings through application of his advanced scientific knowledge. These beings, like Eliza, go through the phase of being mere automata, or robots, before becoming fully alive, at which point one of them kills Pygmalion. In outline, this is very like the story of *Frankenstein* (1818) the fable of modern science written by Mary Shelley (1797–1851)—daughter of the pioneer feminist Mary Wollstonecraft (author of *A Vindication of the Rights of Women*, 1792), and wife of the romantic poet Percy Bysshe Shelley—which has been the basis of innumerable modern plays and horror films. Of course, Eliza does not kill Higgins, but merely throws his slippers at him ('I would have thrown the fire irons', says Mrs Higgins). The suggestion that the recipient does not find the life she has been given altogether good accompanies the presentation of the scientist as an arrogant, presumptuous being who imitates the creative acts of God, and about whose death there lingers a hint of due punishment. Higgins is certainly portrayed as arrogant and presumptuous in the way he takes over Eliza as if she were a worthless object and tries his 'experiment' with her, regardless of what the consequences for her may be.

Since the Renaissance, the outstanding legendary figure taken to represent the human search for a knowledge and power equal to God's has been Faust. The Elizabethan dramatist, Christopher Marlowe (1564–93), and the greatest of German writers, Goethe (1749–1832), were responsible for the most famous literary versions of the Faust legend, in each case linking the pursuit of human perfection with primitive superstitions about black magic, derived from the devil and bringing evil and destruction in its train. The form, or simulacrum, of the most beautiful woman of all time, Helen of Troy, is conjured up for Faust's (in Marlowe's version, Faustus's) delight, and the scholar falls in love with this 'statue'. In Goethe's *Faust*, Part II, Helen is not the only figure of ideal beauty that appears: another is Galatea, whose name has become associated with the statue in modern versions of the Pygmalion story and who is mentioned by Shaw, with reference to Eliza, in the last sentence of his Afterword to *Pygmalion*. Faust's fellow student, Wagner (Pickering is the equivalent in Shaw's play), also creates a new being artificially, a little man. (The poet Shelley whose work was well known to Shaw, translated scenes from Part II of *Faust* into English verse.)

Shaw had a particular interest in yet another legend involving a statue: the legend of Don Juan, which he knew best through the opera, *Don Giovanni* (1787) by Wolfgang Amadeus Mozart (1756–91) but also from *Festin de Pierre* (*The Stone Banquet*) (1665) by Molière (1622–73) and the epic poem, *Don Juan* (1819–24) by George Gordon, Lord Byron (1788–1824). Shaw presented his own version in modern terms in one of his best known plays, *Man and Superman* (1903), but the Don Juan type appears over and over again in his novels and plays and gets frequent mention in his non-fictional writings. The Don Juan of tradition is a seducer of women who eludes capture by any of them, but meets his end through a supernatural vengeance exacted by a statue of the father of one of his victims. Molière represents Don Juan as a rebel against God, a challenger of all laws and conventions. Shaw's Don Juan typically strives to be a philosopher, and to free himself from women and their emotional claims; the form of seduction he indulges in is achieved by persuasive talking and argument which brings the will of others under his control. Certainly Higgins conforms to this type,—and it is his mastery of the art of speech that gives him power over Eliza. What is more, the lengthy dialogues between him and his former pupil, when they are alone together in Acts IV and V, are excellent examples of what one of Shaw's earlier Don Juan characters, Valentine in *You Never Can Tell* (1895–97), calls 'the duel of sex', and indeed they are closely comparable with the verbal exchanges between Valentine and Gloria in that earlier play.

A closer look at Act I brings to light certain details which suggest a supernatural presence of a grander kind than any fairy godmother:

(a) *A blinding flash of lightning, followed instantly by a rattling peal of thunder, orchestrates the incident;*

(b) Higgins's advice to Eliza to 'seek the shelter of some other place of worship', with its allusion to the visual setting beside the church;

(c) his hearing of '*the voice of God, rebuking him for his Pharisaic want of charity to the poor girl*' in the striking of the clock at half-past eleven.

Higgins still has reverence for a greater being than himself, at this point. It is in Act II that he succumbs to the temptation to play the god in others' lives. To this extent he is certainly excessively ambitious, an 'overreacher' like Faust, a rebel against the divinely established order of creation like Molière's Don Juan.

Modern scholarship has established connections between the Faust myth and the Don Juan legend in the cultural tradition of Western Europe.* It is doubtful whether Shaw was objectively aware of the link; and he may even have been unaware that Galatea provided a connection between Pygmalion and Faust. What *Pygmalion* reveals is the dramatist's imaginative grasp of how dominant aspects of modern consciousness are caught up and symbolised in certain key figures from literature. The mythic, or legendary, patterns embedded in Shaw's play operate beneath the surface, and give depth and some variety of emotional relevance to what is superficially light entertainment. They suggest ideas within ideas, further questions lurking unresolved within the more obvious questions. This is, perhaps, the most powerful means Shaw uses to enlarge the scope of his drama, giving its particularities a much more general and profounder relevance.

Themes implied by the various legends

The sources or parallels to *Pygmalion* offered by these stories illustrate certain abstract ideas, or themes, which are thus brought within the

*See J.W. Smeed, *Faust in Literature*, Oxford University Press, London, 1975, pages 161–96

range of Shaw's play:

Source	Parallel themes
the Cinderella story	From rags to riches: the elevation of the lowest to highest position;
the Pygmalion legend	The bringing of the ideal to life (by art);
the Faust legend	Man usurps the power of the Creator (and can expect punishment for doing so);
Don Juan (Shaw's version)	The rebel against established order uses speech and logical argument to defend himself against the emotional claims of women, and to subdue them to his will.

The shaping of the plot

Shaw's choice of incident for representation on stage needs to be sharply distinguished from what was shown in the film. In both media, what comes first has the quality of a prologue, leaving the proper beginning of the action to Act II. Most of the characters in Act I are representative social types and never again appear in the play. Their presence allows Shaw to set Eliza's story in its London context; it also establishes certain aspects of social awareness to which that story can be related, for example:

(a) the Sarcastic Bystander refers to the great difference between the lives of the rich and those of the poor ('Park Lane, for instance. I'd like to go into the Housing Question with you, I would');

(b) most of the group are suspicious of the Notetaker as likely to be connected with the police, whom they regard as harrying the poor in order to protect the rich.

Meanwhile, the background of the church, which has room for all men and women, and the public nature of the scene, gives warning that the play is concerned with society as a whole, not just with a few particular individuals. Interest focuses now on Higgins's demonstration of his powers (and some reminiscence of Faust demonstrating his magic may lurk in the scene). No one escapes untouched by his skill.

As far as the story is concerned, Act I is essentially static; instead, all that goes on among the group outside the church is part of Shaw's animated image of classes and types in the London society of the day. Events begin to move in Act II, from the point where Eliza enters to demand her lessons, and continue through Act III and her first major test. After this, the Cinderella-type story is virtually abandoned, though tokens of it remain as indications of how far from it Shaw is taking his characters. The struggle between Eliza and Higgins now comes to the fore, successive stages of it appearing in Act IV and Act V. This struggle is unresolved at the end. In the second half of the play, narrative interest has given way to a more purely dramatic conflict, not only between persons but between distinct points of view which yield separate truths that we may be able to reconcile, but which the play does not reconcile.

This account neglects Doolittle. Though his first appearance fits into the narrative at an appropriate point, the way he takes the centre of the stage distracts attention temporarily from Eliza and has the effect of stopping the action for a while. The effect is repeated in variant form when he enters in Act V. It is as though Shaw is introducing a pause for thought and discussion at two points in the development of his play. Instead of interweaving a secondary plot involving Doolittle with his main plot concerning Eliza, he has used Doolittle to cut sharply across the main plot on those two occasions. There is an obvious parallel between what happens to Eliza and what happens to her father: both are raised from the dust to some eminence in society, and in each case the change in social status appears visibly in a striking change of costume. As we have seen, Doolittle talks of his position in general terms of class morality. What he says acts as a commentary on Eliza's situation, too, bringing out the general significance Shaw wants us to see in her story. The means whereby the two characters are elevated in society are not the same: Eliza becomes a lady through the acquirement of a new way of speaking, new manners and a new style of behaviour; the sudden acquisition of wealth turns Doolittle into a gentleman. Shaw has established a contrast, as well as a parallel, between father and daughter. The parallel is on class lines; the contrast corresponds to a distinction of sex.

The play of ideas

A movement away from the particular towards the general, and from realistic detail towards the discussion of abstract ideas, is characteristic of many of Shaw's plays. It is never complete, in that Shaw lets his characters stay vivid and full of energy, caught in their particular situation. The ideas he raises have topical relevance, but his drama is never reduced to being propaganda for Socialism, or propaganda for or against feminism. He claimed that what he wanted at the Court

Theatre was 'a pit of philosophers', and his plays are designed to set audiences thinking about principles in an objective, dispassionate way. (In many respects, Shaw was the precursor and master of the political dramatist, Bertolt Brecht. Shaw himself thought of the philosophical dialogues of the Athenian philosopher Plato (428/7–348/7 BC) as the ultimate model for his plays.)

The problem of equality

Mrs Higgins comments, in Act III, that 'when Eliza walked into Wimpole Street, something walked in with her, and that 'something' was: 'A problem'. Shaw's aside, '*unconsciously dating herself by the word*', indicates to the reader that he has in mind something beyond the limited, immediate sense in which Mrs Higgins uses the word; and contemporary audiences were likely to have been reminded of a type of play (then rather out-of-date) that had concerned itself specifically with social problems. Shaw flourishes the term, by the way Mrs Higgins speaks it, and so makes it a formal announcement that there is an abstract question to be debated which his play presents, or illustrates, in some way.

Doolittle's answer to 'middle class morality' has the effect of making us consider the habits of the poor as an alternative to middle-class behaviour, and not as a failure to live up to middle-class standards. Already in Act II he himself talks to Higgins as an equal ('You and me is men of the world, aint we?'), regardless of the differences in their social and economic circumstances. As Eliza's father, he openly regards her as inferior to himself; and, though Higgins protests verbally ('Do you mean to say that you would sell your daughter for £50?'), he himself has been treating the girl as an inanimate object without feelings or intelligence, a 'thing', and he does in effect buy her from Doolittle for five pounds. The dustman's advice to Higgins to 'wallop' Eliza with a strap to keep her in order does more than indicate that she appears to both of them as subhuman, an animal around the house, 'a monkey' not yet evolved into a human being (according to the popular notion of Darwin's theory of evolution); it links this way of regarding her with the laws under which women were denied equality with men, not treated as persons in their own right, but as the property of father or husband. Shaw is insinuating the thought that the inequality of the sexes in contemporary society is even greater than inequality between classes.

Ladies and gentlemen

Eliza has to be made into a lady. Higgins's success destroys the assumption that ladies can only be born, and that they are always the products of nature working through natural selection and the inheritance of character. Mrs Eynsford Hill is a lady of that sort, but her daughter, brought up in genteel poverty, is distinctly less of a lady than the flower girl becomes. Of course, Shaw does not prove his point that the lady is a product of culture by straightforward logic or scientific evidence. He does not even quote the famous traditional slogan of English revolutionaries:

> When Adam delved and Eve span,
> Who was then the gentleman?*

Instead, he presents the idea in the form of a fable with strikingly unrealistic elements. However, alongside the fantastic notion that Higgins transforms the 'squashed cabbage leaf', picked up in Covent Garden, by magic, there runs the more credible idea that education can do the trick; and the play does not need to produce undeniable evidence for this, as readers and audiences can find it in society, in the actual world they live in.

The feminist revolt

It is interesting to reflect that the common phrase, 'one of nature's gentlemen', has no equivalent applicable to women. Shaw's play suggests an explanation for this: it takes a man to turn a woman into a lady; in a patriarchal society women are what men make of them, and the lady is the product of male social and sexual idealisations combined in one person. But Galatea was rapidly coming to life in Edwardian England and tossing the slippers, those tokens of domesticity and wifely submissiveness, at her master; even tossing the fire irons, in some instances. Women had organised themselves in a campaign for the right to vote. Ladies became unladylike, demonstrated publicly, resisted the police, and went on hunger strikes when they were thrown into prison. Since the invention of the typewriter, respectable middle-class women had found a way of earning their own living that made them economically independent of their families,—though not independent of employers who were almost without exception male.

Doolittle as gentleman

The millionaire's bequest is enough to bring Doolittle within range of polite society, where he gains acceptance for his personal qualities. (Shaw can justly be charged with underestimating the strength of snobbery in British society to suit his purpose here.) Instead of rejoicing at his good fortune, as convention leads us to expect, Doolittle miserably

---

* 'delved' means 'dug', and 'span' is an old form of the past tense of the verb 'to spin'

laments his new state as very much worse than his previous condition of 'undeserving poverty':

> It's making a gentleman of me that I object to ... I was happy. I was free. I touched pretty nigh everybody for money when I wanted it ... Now I am worrited; tied neck and heels; and everybody touches me for money.

The claims of others on his generosity force him into a travesty of virtue: 'I have to live for others and not for myself'. Worst of all, his fear of poverty now that he is no longer poor, has turned him into a fearful and helpless conformist: 'Intimidated: thats what I am'. Intimidation, as he sees it, is what keeps society as it is: 'We're all intimidated'.

Eliza as lady

These still sound like the exaggerations of a comedian. Eliza's exclamation, 'Oh God! I wish I was dead', in the evening after her triumph, (Act IV) has a very different, more genuinely despairing ring. It can be explained to some extent as an emotional response to Higgins's neglect of her; but the feeling that wells up in her towards the end of the play has clear implications of a less limited and less personal kind:

> Oh! if I only could go back to my flower basket! I should be independent of both you and father and all the world! Why did you take my independence from me? Why did I give it up? I'm a slave now, for all my fine clothes.

The anxieties of Mrs Pearce and Mrs Higgins about Eliza's future, when Higgins and Pickering shall have tired of playing with her as their 'doll', reflect on the weakness and helplessness of any lady with 'the manners and habits that disqualify a fine lady from earning her own living' (Mrs Higgins's words in Act III). In terms of the re-enactment of the fable of Pygmalion's statue, Eliza's 'Not bloody likely' is the stroke that breaks the chain binding her to her master and his intention, demolishes the mould of the lady to let the woman breathe, and for a moment brings a degree of release to the other ladies, also ('Such bloody nonsense', echoes Clara; 'positively reeking with the latest slang', her mother protests; 'you must be perfectly cracked about her', Mrs Higgins declares). But the realistic development of the play continues, and Higgins's rigorous training of his pupil strengthens its hold, until he makes the suggestion that she should provide for herself in ladylike fashion by marrying. Eliza reflects:

> We were above that at the corner of Tottenham Court Road ... I sold flowers. I didnt sell myself. Now youve made a lady of me I'm not fit to sell anything else. I wish youd left me where you found me.

Her view of the middle-class institution of marriage is as disillusioned as her father's.

Male versus female

The conflict between Eliza and Higgins that occupies most of Act IV is set off by his indifference that provokes, first, her savage anger ('I wanted to smash your face. I'd like to kill you, you selfish brute') and then a desire to make him show he cares for her that is gratified by his self-pitying complaint, 'You have wounded me to the heart'. By running away from Wimpole Street, she alarms him to an extent he cannot later deny and, when the struggle between them is resumed in the later part of Act V, Higgins shows himself intensely aware of Eliza, but equally intent on defending his bachelor state against her emotional designs on him. He does this by shifting to higher, more impersonal ground. He justifies himself against the imputation that his manners are inferior to Pickering's by pleading an ideal of radical equality:

> The great secret, Eliza, is not having bad manners or good manners, but having the same manner for all human souls: in short, behaving as if you were in Heaven, where there are no third-class carriages, and one soul is as good as another.

He turns other personal appeals aside in a similar way:

ELIZA	HIGGINS
(a) 'you dont care a bit for me';	'I care for life, for humanity';
(b) 'I wont care for anybody that doesnt care for me';	'Commercial principles ... I am expressing my righteous contempt for Commercialism';
(c) 'You never thought of the trouble it would make for me';	'Would the world ever have been made without making trouble? Making life means making trouble';
(d) 'I notice that you dont notice me';	'I go my way and do my work without caring twopence what happens to either of us'.

Eventually he confronts her with alternatives to choose between: 'the life of the gutter ... warm ... violent'; or 'Science and Literature and Classical Music and Philosophy and Art'. The whole scene is built up on this dialectical patterning through the oppositions of personal to impersonal, emotion to intellect, nature to culture and, by implication, low to high.

The case against Higgins

Higgins does not have matters all his own way in the argument. His persistent feeling that he owns Eliza leaves him open to attack, and so she is able to make him jealous of Freddy. In the revised text of the play, she turns on him with a shrewd comment on his manipulative attitude to people:

> I never thought of us making anything of one another; and you never think of anything else. I only want to be natural.

Eliza's concern, after all, is with living, and Higgins's (like Pygmalion's) more with art and high principles. Her motives and emotions are transparent, but in Higgins she has a dangerous playmate, as she well knows:

> You want me back only to pick up your slippers and put up with your tempers and fetch and carry for you;
>
> You can twist the heart in a girl as easy as some could twist her arms to hurt her;
>
> you know very well that youre nothing but a bully;
>
> you turn round and make up to me now that I'm not afraid of you.

His ulterior motives, his undoubted egotism and care for his own comfort, and the evidence of how he coaxes Mrs Pearce and plays the part of a spoilt child with her and with his mother, come close to undermining the effect of his enlightened words recommending to Eliza a less personal and more philosophic view of human life. She taunts him with the charge that he is 'a born preacher', implying that fine words are easily spoken but may not be supported by matching actions.

Shaw's irony

Irony is a major stylistic feature to which some writers are particularly addicted. It may be difficult to detect, as its essence is a deceptive simplicity. In recognising irony, the reader or listener perceives that the author is not being entirely frank about his opinions or attitudes which are certainly more complex than he admits and may be opposite to what he expresses. Thus an ironic way of writing demands alertness from the reader and forces him to judge and interpret for himself, instead of relying altogether on the author—who is not to be trusted. The philosopher Socrates emerges as a supreme ironist in the Dialogues of Plato.

Because of Shaw's use of irony it is possible to take the whole of the last part of Act V of Shaw's *Pygmalion* in either of two ways. On the one hand, we can read the dialogue between Higgins and Eliza as completing the re-enactment of the Pygmalion legend by prompting the girl through the final stages of her development to the point where he exclaims: 'By George, Eliza, I said I'd make a woman of you; and I have', and offers her the fullest respect he is capable of showing:

> Now youre a tower of strength: a consort battleship. You and I and Pickering will be three old bachelors instead of two old men and a silly girl.

But it is noticeable that this last speech ignores her proposal to marry Freddy and indeed excludes that young man from any part in the future Higgins is imagining. Even more ominously, he reverts to treating Eliza as a servant for his own convenience just before the play ends. It seems that the entire scene may, alternatively, be a demonstration of how a selfish man can maintain his domination over women. The film version ends with Higgins roaring with laughter. Certainly that is an appropriate ending for a comedy, and the audience may well join in with him. But, equally, they may be left uncomfortably speculating on what exactly amuses him so much. Shaw ironically leaves the play open to our interpretation. We should, perhaps, recognise again the truth of Doolittle's comment that there is 'a little of both' honest man and rogue in everyone, and be prepared to take whatever degree of wisdom we can find in Higgins's words, but to reject any notion of him as a fount of wisdom, or an impartial commentator on anything in the play. Instead of giving us the answers, Shaw makes us think and judge for ourselves.

Vital genius

Higgins thinks very well of himself and contemptuously of commoner souls and fools, including Freddy. Yet he asserts that 'one soul is as good as another'. Shaw wrote elsewhere of 'vital geniuses' and portrayed the type especially in *Saint Joan* (1923) and *The Millionairess* (1934). Eliza, even as a flower seller, certainly shows this quality of genius. So does her father. It could be argued that it is this, rather than chance or Higgins's work alone, that carries them both out of their original class into a higher. Higgins, too, with his energy, enthusiasm and skill, is another vital genius, and he proves it, thereby winning his bet. In fact, Shaw has left the problem of equality unresolved in this respect. Can we reconcile the observation that people in society are not equal in their qualities and accomplishments with the idea of 'having the same manner for all human souls'? Shaw demonstrates through Higgins and Eliza that women remain different from men in attitude and personality even when they achieve equality with them; he leaves us still to ponder on what equality really means.

The characters

Eliza, Higgins and Alfred Doolittle are the major characters in the play; all the rest are minor, less memorable than those three, as they are not individualised in the same detail.

Alfred Doolittle

Doolittle belongs to a different category from all the others. He is more immediately recognisable as a stage character, not realistically presented to give the effect of an actual human being. In performance, the part is like a mask that the actor wears: with simpler, more boldly drawn lines than we find in an actual human face. Furthermore, what he says matches what he is with an exactness and completeness we should not expect to find in real people. He is the spokesman for that section of the lower classes he refers to as 'the undeserving poor', and he is much more clear-sighted and articulate in talking about the values and beliefs of such people than any actual members of this sub-class are likely to be (a point that Shaw recognises and turns to account in his plot, by having Doolittle's extraordinariness recognised by the bequest of a small fortune, on condition that he gives public lectures). In fact, Doolittle makes explicit in his words what Shaw has seen implied in the behaviour of the 'undeserving poor'.

Shaw has made the character attractive and amusing, whereas a realistically presented drunkard who beat up his daughter and cared nothing for her, and who preferred blackmailing gentlemen to earning money by working, would very probably be repugnant to us; or, if treated sympathetically, would be a pathetic or even tragic character. It is Doolittle's frankness and lack of shame, and his self-confident ease in the company of very different people, that make him attractive in Act II. These are all positive characteristics suggestive of good health and good temper, as such negative characteristics as self-consciousness, fear and guilt never are.

We laugh *with* Doolittle in Act II; we laugh *at* him in Act V. For on his second appearance, he asks for sympathy and appears somewhat pathetic. The recognition that this character is not real, but a device of the author's, controls the degree of pathos he arouses and allows us still to laugh. Indeed we laugh all the more because the sharp contrast between Doolittle in Act V and Doolittle in Act II is very unlikely, and because we are at least vaguely aware of the paradox that this character is happy in circumstances that would make most people miserable, and he is miserable in circumstances that would bring joy to others.

His appearances stand out in the structure of the play like turns by a comedian or a clown put on in the intervals of a continuing play.

Eliza

In Act I the flower girl whom we know later as Eliza Doolittle seems rather like a heroine in a melodrama, a favourite nineteenth-century type of play which encouraged audiences to indulge their emotions and presented its heroines (often poor girls) as helpless innocents in distress, claiming the audience's pity. A cliché describing such heroines was: 'She was poor, but she was honest'. The flower girl describes herself as 'a poor girl' and keeps insisting that she is 'a respectable girl', meaning 'honest'. She is, in fact, seeing herself as this conventional type of character, but is also capable of exaggerating the impression she makes, as if deliberately playing a role. Thus, when the crowd starts reacting with pleased interest to Higgins's display of skill, she does not respond with them but remains apart, repeating her grievances over and over:

Aint no call to meddle with me, he aint;

He's no gentleman, he aint, to interfere with a poor girl;

He's no right to take away my character.

She even speaks of herself in the third person:

Poor girl! Hard enough for her to live without being worried and chivied.

Such insistent self-pity is unattractive, and Higgins is extremely irritated by it. But suspicion that Eliza may not really be like this, but just acting, is raised when she is caught out in a lie:

Buy a flower, kind gentleman. I'm short for my lodging.

('Liar. You said you could change half-a-crown', is Higgins's response.) When she has a handful of gold and silver coins to put in her purse, she appears quite different: cheeky, bold, proud of herself; and her spirit attracts the taxi driver's admiration. It appears that the distortion of character was related to Eliza's poor circumstances; when these change, so does she.

Through the rest of the play, Shaw presents the gradual development of Eliza's character, and she seems most natural and least comic when she has turned into a lady. It is at this stage that the character betrays genuine feelings which touch us, instead of showing off false or exaggerated feelings. There is a quiet desperation in her that prompts us to think more gravely about the plight of the lady in Edwardian society, and the plight of women in relation to men. In place of her earlier self-pity, she shows a genuine modesty in comparing her ignorance with the learning of Higgins and Pickering. Vanity and boastfulness turn into self-respect and a demand for fair treatment that becomes justifiably aggressive in reaction to Higgins's treatment of her. We can perceive a consistency in Eliza's character, a continuity from Act I to Act V, despite the evident changes.

Higgins

Higgins is the clown of the play. He is full of tricks and antics which are amusing to watch. Shaw comments explicitly on the fact that he is like a spoilt baby. His bursts of temper, his generally noisy behaviour, his egotistic sense of his own importance, his careless untidiness, his rudeness, his self-indulgence (indicated at the very beginning of Act II by the presence of the dish piled up with fruit and chocolates), are all childish features. He does not seem to know himself at all well; certainly he does not recognise himself in Mrs Pearce's view of him. His energy comes across very strongly, through his restless physical movements; the swift and ready movements of his mind that enable him to outwit others and get his own way all the time; through his verbal readiness and fluency; and, not least, through the assertive vigour of his style of speech with its swift twists and turns, its exaggerations, and its constant use of slangy expressions or striking and usually comic metaphors and similes. We accept the fact that he is exceptionally clever at his job, but this is not an excuse for his arrogance and vanity, for the way he exploits women, or his readiness with lies and other forms of deceitful behaviour to further his own ends. As with Doolittle, it is partly the comic treatment that enables us to like a character with so many vices. Eliza's and Mrs Higgins's interest in him and affection for him also help us to see Higgins as a likeable person. His self-dramatising postures, and the exaggerated way in which he expresses his reactions, convey a sense that there is a real Higgins hidden behind all the play-acting bluster. At times, we may suspect that the hidden self is benevolent, generous and trustworthy; at other times, we may suspect this self of being treacherous and entirely selfish.

It is possible to see Higgins as Shaw's satirical portrait of himself, and to see the Professor's cat-and-mouse game with Eliza, in Act V, as a reflection of the dramatist's evasive flirtation with Mrs Patrick Campbell, the actress who played Eliza in 1914. In so far as Higgins stands for Pygmalion, the artist, he must also represent the dramatist, whose play is the product of a creative process and will, when finished, stand independent of him. The laughing figure of Higgins then stands at the end of the screen version like the signature of the author, or of his Muse of Comedy.

The minor characters

Colonel Pickering gives the impression of being an ideal gentleman, though he is not drawn in any detail. He has served his country overseas;

he is always courteous to women, and his politeness is not just a style, but conveys true respect; and he is thoroughly trustworthy. He is also older than Higgins, and the correctness of his manners makes him seem rather old-fashioned and conservative. As Higgins's fellow scholar, Wagner to the other's Faust, he can be roused to an enthusiasm that makes him lose sight of realities temporarily. The bachelorhood of the pair enables Shaw to suggest that intellect flourishes most when women are kept at a distance and the emotional claims of love and the responsibilities of marriage can be avoided. The comradeship of Pickering and Higgins contrasts with the turbulent relationship between Higgins and Eliza; but on the whole Pickering's presence in the play serves to set off the character of Higgins by contrast.

Mrs Higgins is the ideal mother, wise, tolerant, caring for others, yet self-contained, detached and contented in her quiet, orderly life. Her room expresses her sense of beauty and testifies to her culture. Altogether she is a figure of stability and comfort and her presence in the play acts as a guarantee that nothing will go seriously wrong.

Mrs Pearce, Higgins's housekeeper, belongs to the respectable lower classes that, through close contact as servants to their social superiors, have come to adopt middle-class standards of behaviour and morality. Her concern with cleanliness and tidiness is partly a mark of her profession, and partly characteristic of a mother looking after a small boy, which seems to be her principal role in Higgins's bachelor household. This character is defined almost exclusively in terms of the way she relates to the others in the household.

Mrs Eynsford Hill is a less vivid portrait of an older lady than we have in Mrs Higgins. This is a comment on her personality as well as on Shaw's delineation of her. She is more conventional than Mrs Higgins, and only comes to life as a human being in those moments when she speaks as the anxious mother, concerned about Eliza's seeming to know Freddy, in Act I, and apologising to Mrs Higgins for Clara, and seeking her approval of Freddy, in Act III.

Clara is the most individualised member of her family. She is brash and clumsy in society, stronger-willed than her mother and her brother, both of whom she tends to nag and scold. By contrast with her, Eliza's natural grace and sensitiveness shine more brightly, but Clara is not without spirit, and the improvement in her that Shaw describes in the Afterword begins in the play with her imitation of Eliza.

We see little of **Freddy** except a stereotype of the foolish and futile young-man-about-town. He may be good-hearted, but he is good for nothing apart from his love for Eliza. Indeed, falling in love, which makes most people look foolish, is the brightest thing Freddy does. His failure to get a taxi, in Act I, is a pointer towards his uselessness. Clara's crossness may make us feel a little sorry for him, but Freddy proves that men can be weaker than women, less competent, less capable of independence. Eliza recognises that, if she marries Freddy, she will have to support him.

The dialogue

Although Shaw has used a considerable amount of Cockney dialect and slang in *Pygmalion*, the general style of the dialogue does not attempt to capture actual conversational habits accurately, but is artfully designed for literary and stage effect. The characters usually speak in complete sentences, not in broken phrases and monosyllables, and the major characters sometimes deliver quite long speeches which are thoroughly fluent and carefully constructed to give them maximum force. Certainly, the long speeches given to Higgins and Eliza come in scenes where feeling is running high, and it can be argued that passionate feeling can make human beings more than usually eloquent,—if it does not reduce them to speechlessness. But strictly naturalistic plays tend to keep to a bare form of dialogue (and Ibsen's social plays have sometimes been criticised for this). Shaw, on the other hand, shares frankly with his audiences a consciousness that his plays are works of art to be presented as theatrical entertainment, and so he freely accepts traditional conventions of the theatre, especially the freedom to write as rhetorically as Shakespeare did.

Of course, unlike Shakespeare, Shaw does not write in verse, but the dialogue of *Pygmalion* is written in a very stylish prose, as full of colour and variety as poetry. The Cockney element adds to the expressive richness of the play and contributes to the amusement of the audience. The slang and the swearing give vigour and add to the variety of tone employed. Higgins's speech, as befits a linguist, shows greatest differentiation from the speech of the other characters and the greatest stylistic range. He himself comments on Doolittle's natural use of balanced, alliterative phrases. His own speech is much more rapid in tempo and flexible in its rhythms, following the often ingenious movement of his thought, as well as frequently employing hyperbole and other figurative expressions. Shaw's plays are powerful reminders that he had served an apprenticeship as a public speaker in the cause of Socialism.

Part 4

Hints for study

THE FOLLOWING NOTES assume that the study of *Pygmalion* is an end in itself, not a means to understanding something else, such as the nature of English society, or the personality of the author. Their aim is to help the student to understand and enjoy the play as fully as possible. This is the soundest basis for passing examinations.

It will be helpful to keep certain general considerations in mind. Firstly, there is no single right interpretation of any text; the better we get to know the work, the more we are likely to find in it. Yet false interpretations are certainly possible and need to be avoided by attentive reading and re-reading to ensure that:

What the author has written is understood accurately;

as little as possible is overlooked or forgotten;

the different parts of the whole are seen in relation to each other.

Secondly, allowance must be made for the fact that *Pygmalion* is a play, written originally for performance in a theatre. Though the descriptions of settings and characters that Shaw included in the printed text do much to limit the disadvantages of having to read rather than see and hear the play, it is necessary to try to consider continually what would be seen on the stage, and how the dialogue would sound. For example, if the setting of Act I is kept in mind (and Shaw wanted producers to keep as close as they could to the scale of the actual St Paul's Church in the stage set), its grandeur will suggest that the play is concerned with something greater than the immediate trivialities of the dialogue; or being aware of Higgins's restless movements in the later acts will add appreciably to a sense of what the character is like. Imagining different voices speaking the lines will banish any sense of monotony and increase awareness of the differences between the characters, and of conflicts and contrasts between them.

In this connection there is one general warning to be given: avoid concluding that what any character says represents the author's opinion. Occasionally a dramatist may employ one of his characters as his own spokesman, but it takes great skill and experience as a reader of plays to detect any passages where this occurs, and the student will never go seriously wrong in doubting whether anything less than the entire play reflects the author's view. Attention has already been drawn to the way in which Eliza's responses undercut the effect of Higgins's wise-sounding speeches in Act V and make us look critically at him.

Finally, it is unwise to jump to conclusions about any part of the text until you are satisfied that you have a good grasp of the whole.

Organising your study

After reading the play through and mastering the contents of each act in a general way, it is a good plan to increase your grasp of the work by turning your attention from the details to discover the structure and themes.

Structure and plot

Both these terms are applied to the author's arrangement of his material in the work as a whole, which gives it a particular form or design.

In looking for the plot, it is necessary to identify the connected series of events whereby the situation at the beginning of the play is changed to the situation at the end. (In discussions of drama, this is sometimes called the action, or action plot.) The plot of *Pygmalion* certainly concentrates on Eliza and Higgins. Looking at Acts II, III, IV and V, we can sum up the plot as follows:

Eliza seeks out Higgins, is bought by him, and her education starts.—Part of the way through her training, Higgins tries an experiment with Eliza that is not altogether successful.—After a later, entirely successful experiment, the pupil turns against the teacher.—Further struggles take place between them, resulting in an adjustment in their relationship.

This summary takes no account of Act I. What event, or events, in Act I link up with the other items in the summary? Can you see why Act I might be described as a prologue to the play, largely or entirely outside the plot proper?

You probably feel some dissatisfaction with the plot summary just given. It is not what you would have written and may well leave out some elements that seem to you important. Now write down your own version of the plot in roughly the same number of words as are used above. If you are still not entirely happy, try writing yet another version. This will make you realise that even the plot of the play can be looked at in various ways that do not cancel each other out.

Note that any part of the story reflected in the play that is not actually written up for stage presentation does not count as part of the plot. Eliza's appearance at the party where she is mistaken for a princess is the obvious high point of the story, but Shaw has not chosen to include it and so make it the main climax of his play. (If you have read the film script, try to think of the play as it was without the additions for the screen.)

What seems to you to be the main climax, or chief turning-point, of the whole play? If you have difficulty in deciding this, see if you can identify the climax of each separate Act.

If we think in terms of **structure**, we are still looking for ways in which the dramatist arranges his material, but we are now not only or mainly concerned with the line of the play's development from the first act to the end. We are likely to be more concerned with what are sometimes called 'spatial' arrangements as distinct from the arrangement of happenings in a temporal sequence. (A prologue outside the plot is part of the structure of the whole play.) It is quite likely that you were dissatisfied with the plot summary that made no mention of Doolittle. It is possible to describe his two appearances in the play as elements in the structure that interrupt the line of development of the plot. As there is a very marked change in Doolittle at his second appearance, it could be said that there is a suggestion of a **second action plot** in the play, concerned with what happens to Doolittle, not with what happens to Eliza and Higgins. This minimal secondary plot (minimal because we are shown only two stages of Doolittle's story) is linked with the main plot through Doolittle's relationship with Eliza. However, we could also say that the parallel between what happens to Doolittle and what happens to Eliza seems more significant in the structure of the play than the realistic detail of blood-relationship.

Can you see any other, slighter parallels or contrasts between two characters in the play?

Higgins and Pickering are an obvious pair of characters. Turn to the first section of Act V and make notes on the differences between them that Eliza is anxious to point out.

Now consider the difference between the relationship of Doolittle and Eliza and the relationship of Mrs Higgins and her son. Compare the relationship of (a) Mrs Eynsford Hill to Clara and (b) Mrs Eynsford Hill to Freddy with (c) the other parent-child relationships in the play. (The placing of minor characters in relation to major characters is part of the structure.)

Other large scale patterns contributing to the total structure include the repetition of scenes, or passages, in variant forms, for example:

(i) Doolittle's first and second visits;

(ii) the conflict between Eliza and Higgins in the last section of Act IV and, again, in the last section of Act V.

Similar effects at widely separated moments in the play may link different scenes, for example:

   (*i*) Doolittle's surprise at seeing Eliza clean and dressed in the kimono (Act II);
   (ii) Eliza's surprise at seeing her father dressed as a gentleman (Act V).

Can you find any other major, or minor, parallels of this kind?

Devices of arrangement bring variety into the play. Extremely effective in this respect is the way in which the dialogue is distributed among the characters. Shaw was especially concerned with the quality of the actors' voices when casting his plays for performance. He wanted to avoid monotony by having all the characters sound very different from each other and yet, between them, covering a wide range of pitch and tone. Notice how he breaks up each act into passages involving different pairs, or groups, of characters, and varies duologues between only two characters with ensemble passages drawing in four or more speakers. Look at each act to see how it is broken up in this way and you will find that Act IV stands out in contrast to the rest, as it is divided simply into two duologues: (*i*) Higgins and Pickering and (*ii*) Higgins and Eliza. This gives special emphasis to Act IV and may help with the decision as to where the central point, or climax, of the play comes.

Variety is also introduced through the alternating of:

   (*a*) passages mainly concerned with dramatising the story, or continuing the action plot; with
   (*b*) passages given up to discussion of more abstract questions, or that seem to act as a commentary on questions raised in the plot.

Notice where the two types of passage come in relation to each other. Do you find type (*b*) occurring more frequently in the second half of the play?

This brings us to the next main consideration of any study.

Theme

Any story is given meaning and relevance to other men's experience in the world by the way that the author writes it. Discovering the theme of any work involves becoming aware of generalisations arising out of the specific story, characters and settings of the work. Such general reflections may be:

   (*a*) explicit in the dialogue (as in Doolittle's comments on class habits and morality); or (*b*) indirectly implied in the patterning of the work, through such devices as repetition, or the presentation of analogies (as when Eliza's appearance as a lady is followed later in the play by Doolittle's appearance as a gentleman); or

(*c*) implied through the reflection of an actual social context in the work (as the realistic setting of the play in Edwardian London invites us to make connections with actual class distinctions and the wide gulf between rich and poor, in contemporary England, and with the feminists' demand for equality with men) or

(*d*) prompted by allusions contained in the play (as in Shaw's choice of *Pygmalion* as a title, and in his reminders of the Cinderella story).

Most works of any serious value have more than one theme, and some of these may have emerged in the process of writing without the author's prior intention. Shaw was anxious to make people think about the society in which they lived, and so he made the stories he presented yield many ideas. (This is a considerable element in his skill). Themes discoverable in *Pygmalion* include:

(*i*) class distinctions

(*ii*) distinctions (social and natural) between men and women

(*iii*) the concept of the lady/gentleman

(*iv*) vital genius

(*v*) education

(*vi*) the educator as a power in society

(*vii*) tyranny and slavery

(*viii*) the conflict between intellect and emotion

(*ix*) the 'duel of sex', or fundamental conflict between male and female

(*x*) the power of the scientist (who practises objective detachment, and loyalty to abstract principles) over ordinary, more instinctual human beings

You may be able to add more. You will certainly recognise some of these themes more quickly than others, and feel that some are more important in the play than others. You will also notice that some of these separate themes can be grouped together as aspects of larger themes. Several are concerned with equality or inequality.

See how many of the listed themes you can illustrate with at least one reference to a particular aspect of the play, or passage in the play, or even quotation. For example:

(*iii*) THE CONCEPT OF THE LADY:

(*a*) the plot traces the transformation of a poor Cockney flower girl into a fine lady;

(b) Eliza, talking to Pickering in Act V for Higgins's benefit, gives two definitions of what makes a lady:

'it was from you that I learnt really nice manners; and that is what makes one a lady, isnt it?'

'the difference between a lady and a flower girl is not how she behaves, but how she's treated';

(c) Mrs Higgins, in Act III, sees that being a lady can have disadvantages as well as advantages:

'The manners and habits that disqualify a fine lady from earning her own living without giving her a fine lady's income!'

(d) Higgins, earlier in Act III, has implied that there is little difference between ladies and gentlemen and the rest of humanity: 'we're all savages, more or less. We're supposed to be civilized and cultured—to know all about poetry and philosophy and art and science, and so on; but how many of us know even the meaning of these names'.

(iv) VITAL GENIUS:

(a) in Act I, Eliza shows much more spirit than Freddy and plays the fine lady riding in a carriage to Buckingham Palace with a degree of imagination and enjoyment that win the taxi driver's admiration;

(b) Higgins, in Act II, responds to Eliza's enterprise in offering to pay for lessons:

'She offers me two-fifths of her day's income
for a lesson ... It's handsome. By George,
it's enormous! it's the biggest offer I ever had';

(c) the dustman is left a fortune in recognition of the fact that he is 'the most original moralist at present in England';

(d) Higgins says to Eliza, in Act V:

'it's quite true that your father ... will be quite at home in any station of life to which his eccentric destiny may call him'.

The general style of the play

Identifying this is very necessary if misunderstanding and faulty judgement of the play are to be avoided. For instance, Shaw describes *Pygmalion* as 'A Romance' and explains his use of the term as an indication that it is not a realistic play in its presentation of what happens to Eliza (and her father).

We have noticed that it is like a fairy story in some ways, and that it contains traces of mythic quality in the way it recalls the legend of Pygmalion and Faust's impious attempts to take on God's privilege of creation, through his use of (evil) magic arts. So it would be wrong to criticise the play for not being realistic, instead of recognising that Shaw gives his story great richness of significance by these departures from realism. Yet the settings are realistic and (a) help us to become interested in the characters as if they were real people, and (b) allow us to interpret the play as relevant in some respects to contemporary social questions. This blend of styles is apparent in the character-drawing, too: the extent to which Doolittle belongs to a non-realistic convention of character-drawing has been discussed in Part 2; and the balance Shaw achieves between making the other characters psychologically convincing (as in presenting Higgins's relationship with his mother as background to his bachelordom) and effective stage characters who can deliver long speeches without offending against our sense of realism.

Evidence from outside the play

Knowledge of facts of the author's life, the social conditions of his time, his cultural background, and the background of the public he originally wrote for, can be helpful to an understanding of the play, and can enrich our reading of it. Knowing that Shaw was a convinced Socialist will help us to avoid the mistake of supposing that *Pygmalion* is meant to encourage poor people with hopes of rising in society if they take the opportunity to educate themselves. Part 1 of these Notes has pointed out the intense snobbery in Shaw's family background, and knowing this can make us more keenly aware of his concern with the question of equality, and aware of the conflicts, between a sense of superiority (or personal distinction) and Socialist principles, that are still present in the play and contribute to its lively, dynamic effect. A reading of Act I is helped by some knowledge of the nature of the various localities named, and the class of people living there. Recognising that Pickering's club, the Carlton, places him as a Conservative (or Tory) in politics, alerts us to a suspicion that the Socialist author may not consider Pickering's form of respect to ladies as leading to the long-term welfare of women.

Some acquaintance with other works by the same author may help confirm an interpretation of the play, or make us hesitate to accept it. This form of additional knowledge certainly aids quick recognition of the general style of the work, and the identification of incidental artistic devices. It also enlarges and confirms our sense of the author's cultural background; thus it is the basis of the suggestion in this book that Higgins's mixed attitude to Eliza, in the later part of the play, reveals him as Shaw's version of Don Juan (bringing in another allusion to a legend well known in Western Europe).

Warning: In writing essays about the play, the student must be careful not to bring in pieces of background information for their own sake, but only when they explain something in the play, or add to the understanding or enjoyment of it.

Enjoying the play

Judging the art of a writer involves seeing how he has made his work enjoyable. If the student can relax enough to enjoy *Pygmalion*, his or her responses make a good basis for study of the dramatist's skill. Ask yourself what you have enjoyed particularly in the play, then look more objectively at what Shaw has said, or how he has arranged things, to give you that pleasure.

Thinking about ideas in the play

One of Shaw's stated aims as a dramatist was to make people think for themselves, sometimes about matters so familiar that they were taken for granted. So part of a true response to his plays is to go on thinking about questions they raise, or ideas they put forward. However, it is necessary for a critical discussion of the work to limit itself carefully to noting lines of thought that the text actually suggests. The student's personal thoughts on subjects raised by the work should not be brought into the discussion if they move in a different direction from the play, or are based on material not contained in the play.

Answering questions on the play

These three processes are involved: (*a*) developing your ideas; (*b*) planning the order of presentation; and (*c*) finding evidence in the text and selecting quotations to illustrate and support your argument.

Examples to consider

QUESTION: *What is your view of Mrs Higgins and her part in the play?*

Asking yourself a number of subsidiary questions may help you to gather ideas for an answer, for example:

(*i*) What is her part in the story? How important is she in it?

(*ii*) In what parts of the play is she on stage, and what kinds of thing does she say and do in these scenes?

(*iii*) What is her attitude to the other characters, particularly to the main characters?

(*iv*) What is she like, and how do you feel about her?

(*v*) What part of society does she represent?

(*vi*) Does she contribute to the general mood and tone of the play?

In putting your answer in order, establish the simpler and more definite facts first, then move gradually to the points arising out of your own sensitive response to the character, and to those involving your judgments about the play as a whole. The result might follow these lines:

Mrs Higgins is the mother of one of the main characters. As she is outside the household at Wigmore Street, Higgins uses her home for the first introduction of Eliza into polite society. Eliza later runs there for advice and protection. She accepts people as they are (Higgins, Eliza, Doolittle); she does what she can to see that those in her home treat each other politely and with consideration; she gives good advice and responds to appeals from others (including Doolittle's request that she go to his wedding). Although she wishes others well, she also judges them shrewdly and objectively (Higgins, Mrs Eynsford Hill). She regards Higgins as rude, tactless and irresponsible in his dealings with other people, and generally childish in his behaviour, apart from his knowledge and skill in his work. She talks to him patiently, but as a mother to a tiresome child; and it is worth noting that she lives independently in her own home, where she is not bothered by him all the time. She sympathises with Eliza and considers that she was fully justified in throwing the slippers at Higgins.

Mrs Higgins seems wise and trustworthy; we respect her and do not dislike her, though she is perhaps too formal and detached for us to feel very warmly towards her. The furnishings of her home suggest that she loves beauty and colour, an aspect of character that is lacking in her son, whose room is bare of colour; it is a comfortable place, not modern and up-to-date, and she is much the same herself.

Her presence in the play supplies a background of stability and acts as an assurance that nothing disastrous will happen in the course of the play. Through her, Shaw guides our attitude to Higgins, leading us to see him as a spoilt child, not to be taken too seriously, or regarded too harshly.

Select a few of Mrs Higgins's speeches, illustrating some of the points made. Aptly placed, they make an answer more vivid and convincing; but do not quote at length: a sentence is more effective than a paragraph, unless you wish to go on and analyse the paragraph closely.

QUESTION: *How does Shaw mark the difference between his characters through their speech?*

The answer might proceed from the general to the particular, on these lines:

(a) Accents and dialects indicate background and class. (Refer to Higgins's demonstration in Act I; quote an example from Eliza in Act II, or one from Doolittle).

(*b*) Use of slang distinguishes the informal, youthful characters from the older, more staid and respectable, and it sets Higgins alongside Eliza and Clara, rather than alongside Pickering and Mrs Higgins.

(*c*) Individual characters have different ways of speaking, for example:

(*i*) **Higgins** swears frequently ('What the devil . . .'; 'How the devil . . .'; 'Damn Mrs Pearce, and damn the coffee, and damn my own folly . . .).

He often uses exclamations and imperatives ('Oh, Lord knows!' 'What! That thing!'; 'Oh Lord! What an evening! What a crew! What a silly tomfoolery!'; 'Put her in the dustbin'; 'Take her away at once'; 'Put out the lights').

He uses sequences of short sentences, often jumping from one point to another, giving the effect of hurry and energy rather than smooth, continuous thought ('I must. Ive a job for you. A phonetic job'; 'What on earth—! Whats the matter? Get up. Anything wrong?'; 'Nonsense! he cant provide for her. He shant provide for her. She doesnt belong to him. I paid him five pounds for her.').

He exaggerates and uses forceful and colourful expressions ('this draggletailed guttersnipe'; 'Hit you! You infamous creature, how dare you accuse me of such a thing? It is you who have hit me. You have wounded me to the heart').

Altogether, Higgins's mode of speech is highly emotional, a very interesting fact to connect with his declared philosophical attitude.

(*ii*) **Doolittle** also uses short sentences and phrases from time to time, but the effect is slowed down by: his use of forms of address ('So help me, Governor, I never did'; 'a little of both, Enry, like the rest of us'), or parenthetic phrases ('Them words is in his blooming will, in which, Henry Higgins, thanks to your silly joking, he leaves me a share in his Pre-digested Cheese Trust').

He prolongs many of his sentences by adding on clauses and phrases without a break ('a share in his Pre-digested Cheese Trust worth four thousand a year on condition that I lecture for his Wannafeller Moral Reform World League as often as they ask me up to six times a year.'). This gives his speech a measured, unhurried quality.

His speeches on 'undeserving poverty' in Act II are formally rhetorical, like those of an old-fashioned, trained public speaker, full of rhetorical questions ('What am I, Governors both? I ask you, what am I?'), examples of

(ii) contd.	balance and contrast ('I dont need less than a deserving man: I need more'), repeated sentence patterns ('I dont need less ... I dont eat less ...'; 'I want a bit of amusement ... I want cheerfulness and a song ...').

Altogether, Doolittle's deliberate, skilful manner of speech gives him dignity, demonstrates his self-confidence, and has a comic effect through its unexpectedness in coming from a presumably uneducated dustman.

Hints for a last question for you to work on:

QUESTION: *Discuss Higgins's attitude to Eliza*

(Is there a difference between his treatment of Eliza and the way he treats his housekeeper? Consider what others say about his attitude to Eliza. Is there any evidence in the play that he is fond of Eliza? What is the basis of his contempt for her in Act II? What does he seem to want of Eliza? How does he respond to her efforts to make him notice her? How does he respond to her running away? Base your conclusions on the play, not on the Afterword; then see if your view is different from what Shaw says in the Afterword, or much the same.)

Some detailed questions

These are designed to help you in your revision of certain parts of the play, and follow its order:

Preface

After reading the Preface, can you explain why it should be 'impossible for an Englishman to open his mouth without making some other Englishman hate or despise him'? (Make some allowance for Shaw's exaggerative style). You may wish to come back to this question after reading through the play.

Act I: First Section

---

(1) How many of the characters' names do we know at this point?
(2) What effect does Shaw get from referring to them all as The Mother, The Bystander, The Flower Girl, The Gentleman, and so on, instead of by their names?
(3) What impression of Clara's character have you gained from this scene? Pick out three or four of the things she says that contribute to this impression. How different is she from her mother?

Act I: Second Section

(1) How would you describe the Flower Girl's behaviour in this act?

(2) What points in her behaviour are connected with her poverty and low-class cultural background? In what ways does she show her self-respect?

(3) Compare Freddy's inability to get a cab with the Flower Girl's commandeering of the one he eventually finds. What does this suggest about the two personalities?

Act II: First Section

(1) What different means has Higgins used to persuade Eliza to do what he wants?

(2) What have you learnt about Higgins's character from this scene? On what evidence is your view of him based?

Act II: Second Section

(1) What is Mrs Pearce's view of Higgins?

(2) What middle class, or upper class, opinions does Alfred Doolittle challenge?

(3) What view of marriage does Doolittle give?

(4) How does Pickering treat Eliza?

(5) How much does Eliza learn during this Act? Does her informal education in Wimpole Street have any bad effects on her?

Act III

(1) Compare Shaw's description of Mrs Higgins's room with his description of her son's laboratory at the beginning of Act II. How are the very different natures of the two people reflected in the furnishings and decorations of their rooms?

(2) Make a note of four ways in which Higgins's behaviour is uncivilised by his mother's standards.

(3) It is generally agreed that incongruity is potentially comic and can set people laughing. What incongruities do you note in Eliza's manner and conduct in Mrs Higgins's drawing room?

(4) Find two ideas expressed by Higgins before Eliza's arrival that are illustrated or confirmed by what happens afterwards.

Act IV

(1) What are Higgins's and Pickering's criticisms of fashionable society?

(2) In what ways does Higgins show his lack of respect for Eliza and his failure to realise how she has changed?

(3) Higgins tries to quieten Eliza by using a number of strategies commonly employed by men in managing women. What are they?

(4) How does Eliza undermine Higgins's image of himself and make him uncomfortable?

(5) What view of marriage does Shaw imply through Higgins's and Eliza's comments in this Act?

Act V

(1) In what ways is the transformation of Alfred Doolittle (*a*) like and (*b*) unlike the transformation of Eliza?

(2) What lessons has Pickering taught Eliza that Higgins could not teach her?

(3) What does Eliza want from Higgins?

(4) What does Higgins want from Eliza?

(5) List any points made in Act V about (*a*) independence and (*b*) equality.

(6) Is Eliza more self-reliant and independent at the end of the play than at the beginning?

(7) Look closely at Doolittle's speeches in Act V and see whether these just confirm his earlier views, or whether anything is added.

Part 5

Suggestions for further reading

The text

The texts of *Pygmalion* used in the preparation of this book were:
- (*a*) the first separate printing of the play, issued by Constable and Company Ltd., London, 1918 (a re-issue of the text first included in the collection, Bernard Shaw, *Androcles and the Lion, Overruled, Pygmalion*, Constable and Company Ltd, London, 1916). The original version for the stage.
- (*b*) the edition first published by Penguin Books Ltd, Harmondsworth, 1941, and reprinted many times since. The film version, illustrated with drawings by Feliks Topolski.
- (*c*) *The Bodley Head Bernard Shaw: Collected Plays with their Prefaces*, edited by Dan H. Laurence, Max Reinhardt, The Bodley Head, London, 1972, volume 4, pages 653–823. The film version without Topolski's drawings, but with the addition of several short documents by Shaw relating to *Pygmalion* and its productions.

Other works by Shaw

Plays relevant to *Pygmalion*:

Back to Methuselah in *The Bodley Head Bernard Shaw: Collected Plays with their Prefaces*, Max Reinhardt, London, 1972, volume 5, pages 251–715; especially the Pygmalion episode, pages 589–604. Also available in the World's Classics series, Oxford University Press, London, 1945.

Man and Superman, Penguin Books, Harmondsworth, 1946; Bantam Books, New York, 1959; and *The Bodley Head Bernard Shaw*, volume 2.

You Never Can Tell, in Bernard Shaw, *Plays Pleasant*, Penguin Books, Harmondsworth, 1946; also in *The Bodley Head Bernard Shaw*, volume 1.

Critical writings:
The Quintessence of Ibsenism, Hill and Wang, New York, 1959; also
   in *Major Critical Essays*, Constable and Company Ltd., London
   1932, part of the Standard Edition of the Works of Bernard Shaw,
   now out of print. (A new edition is planned in continuation of *The
   Bodley Head Bernard Shaw*.)

Letters:
Bernard Shaw and Mrs Patrick Campbell: Their Correspondence,
   edited by Alan Dent, Victor Gollancz, London, 1952. (The letters
   from this collection most relevant to *Pygmalion* will be included in
   volume 3 of *Bernard Shaw: Collected Letters*, edited by Dan H.
   Laurence, Max Reinhardt, London. Volumes 1 and 2 have already
   appeared.)

Works by other authors for comparison with *Pygmalion*

BARKER, HARLEY GRANVILLE *The Madras House* (1910), new edition,
   Eyre Methuen, London, 1977. Closely related to Shaw's play.
FORSTER, E.M. *Howards End* (1910), Penguin Books, Harmondsworth,
   1941. Another view of Edwardian society and its class system.

Life of Shaw

There is no very satisfactory life of Shaw at present. (Michael Holroyd
is at work on the authorised biography.) The most detailed attempts
are:

HENDERSON, ARCHIBALD *Bernard Shaw: Playboy and Prophet*, Appleton
   and Company, New York and London, 1932.
HENDERSON, ARCHIBALD *Bernard Shaw: Man of the Century*, Appleton
   and Company, New York, 1956.

General Studies
BENTLEY, ERIC *Bernard Shaw*, New Directions, Norfolk, Connecticut,
   1947; second edition, Methuen, London, 1967. An intelligent study
   of Shaw's thought.
WILSON, COLIN *Bernard Shaw. A Reassessment*, Hutchinson, London,
   1969.

Other Studies
CARPENTER, CHARLES *Bernard Shaw and the Art of Destroying Ideals*,
   University of Wisconsin Press, Madison, Wisconsin, 1969. An excel-
   lent study of the early plays.

COSTELLO, DONALD *The Serpent's Eye; Shaw and the Cinema*, University of Notre-Dame Press, Notre-Dame, Indiana, 1965. Interesting in connection with the film version of *Pygmalion*.

CROMPTON, LOUIS *Shaw the Dramatist*, University of Nebraska Press, Lincoln, Nebraska; Allen and Unwin, London, 1971.

DUKORE, BERNARD *Bernard Shaw, Director*, University of Washington, Seattle; Allen and Unwin, London, 1971. On Shaw as a producer of his own plays.

GIBBS, A.M. *Shaw* (Writers and Critics series), Oliver and Boyd, Edinburgh and London, 1969. The best short book on Shaw's plays.

KENNEDY, ANDREW *Six Dramatists in Search of a Language*, Cambridge University Press, London, 1975, pages 38–86. A subtle discussion, handicapped by lack of close knowledge of the theatre for which Shaw wrote and insufficient understanding of what he was trying to do.

MAYNE, FRED *The Wit and Satire of Bernard Shaw*, Edward Arnold, London, 1967. A careful, thoroughly illustrated study of Shaw's style on rhetorical lines.

MEISEL, MARTIN *Shaw and the Nineteenth-Century Theatre*, Princeton University Press, New Jersey; Oxford University Press, London, 1963. An exciting book, crammed with information and interesting observations. Useful on the influence of music on Shaw's dramatic writing, as well as on his indebtedness to Victorian melodrama.

MILLS, J.A. *Language and Laughter: Comic Diction in the Plays of Bernard Shaw*, University of Arizona Press, Tucson, Arizona, 1969. Recommended.

MORGAN, MARGERY M. *The Shavian Playground: An Exploration of the Art of George Bernard Shaw*, Methuen, 1972; Methuen University Paperback, 1974. By the author of the present study.

VALENCY, MAURICE *The Cart and the Trumpet*, Oxford University Press, New York, 1973. Includes a different view of *Pygmalion* from the one given in these Notes.

The author of these notes

MARGERY MORGAN was educated at Bedford College, University of London and became a lecturer in medieval literature and modern drama at Royal Holloway College, University of London. She then was a Senior Lecturer, and subsequently Reader in English at Monash University, Melbourne, Australia. She is now emeritus Reader in English and Lecturer in Theatre Studies at the University of Lancaster. Her publications include *A Drama of Political Man: A Study in the Plays of Harley Granville Barker* (1961), and *The Shavian Playground: An Exploration of the Art of G.B. Shaw* (1972). She has edited Shaw's *You Never Can Tell* (1967), and The Devil's Disciple (1983) and Granville Barker's *The Madras House* (1977). Her book on Strindberg was recently published in Macmillan's Modern Dramatist series. She has also written articles on medieval literature and drama, on Shaw, Granville Barker, Strindberg, Australian theatre, and recent English dramatists and is the author of York Notes on *Major Barbara* and the York Handbook *Drama*.

York Notes: list of titles

CHINUA ACHEBE
A Man of the People
Arrow of God
Things Fall Apart

EDWARD ALBEE
Who's Afraid of Virginia Woolf?

ELECHI AMADI
The Concubine

ANONYMOUS
Beowulf
Everyman

JOHN ARDEN
Serjeant Musgrave's Dance

AYI KWEI ARMAH
The Beautyful Ones Are Not Yet Born

W. H. AUDEN
Selected Poems

JANE AUSTEN
Emma
Mansfield Park
Northanger Abbey
Persuasion
Pride and Prejudice
Sense and Sensibility

HONORÉ DE BALZAC
Le Père Goriot

SAMUEL BECKETT
Waiting for Godot

SAUL BELLOW
Henderson, The Rain King

ARNOLD BENNETT
Anna of the Five Towns

WILLIAM BLAKE
Songs of Innocence, Songs of Experience

ROBERT BOLT
A Man For All Seasons

ANNE BRONTË
The Tenant of Wildfell Hall

CHARLOTTE BRONTË
Jane Eyre

EMILY BRONTË
Wuthering Heights

ROBERT BROWNING
Men and Women

JOHN BUCHAN
The Thirty-Nine Steps

JOHN BUNYAN
The Pilgrim's Progress

BYRON
Selected Poems

ALBERT CAMUS
L'Etranger (The Outsider)

GEOFFREY CHAUCER
Prologue to the Canterbury Tales
The Clerk's Tale
The Franklin's Tale
The Knight's Tale
The Merchant's Tale
The Miller's Tale
The Nun's Priest's Tale
The Pardoner's Tale
The Wife of Bath's Tale
Troilus and Criseyde

ANTON CHEKOV
The Cherry Orchard

SAMUEL TAYLOR COLERIDGE
Selected Poems

WILKIE COLLINS
The Moonstone
The Woman in White

SIR ARTHUR CONAN DOYLE
The Hound of the Baskervilles

WILLIAM CONGREVE
The Way of the World

JOSEPH CONRAD
Heart of Darkness
Lord Jim
Nostromo
The Secret Agent
Victory
Youth and *Typhoon*

STEPHEN CRANE
The Red Badge of Courage

BRUCE DAWE
Selected Poems

WALTER DE LA MARE
Selected Poems

DANIEL DEFOE
A Journal of the Plague Year
Moll Flanders
Robinson Crusoe

CHARLES DICKENS
A Tale of Two Cities
Bleak House
David Copperfield
Dombey and Son
Great Expectations
Hard Times
Little Dorrit
Nicholas Nickleby
Oliver Twist
Our Mutual Friend
The Pickwick Papers

EMILY DICKINSON
Selected Poems

JOHN DONNE
Selected Poems

THEODORE DREISER
Sister Carrie

GEORGE ELIOT
Adam Bede
Middlemarch
Silas Marner
The Mill on the Floss

T. S. ELIOT
Four Quartets
Murder in the Cathedral
Selected Poems
The Cocktail Party
The Waste Land

J. G. FARRELL
The Siege of Krishnapur

GEORGE FARQUHAR
The Beaux Stratagem

WILLIAM FAULKNER
Absalom, Absalom!
As I Lay Dying
Go Down, Moses
The Sound and the Fury

HENRY FIELDING
Joseph Andrews
Tom Jones

F. SCOTT FITZGERALD
Tender is the Night
The Great Gatsby

E. M. FORSTER
A Passage to India
Howards End

ATHOL FUGARD
Selected Plays

JOHN GALSWORTHY
Strife

MRS GASKELL
North and South

WILLIAM GOLDING
Lord of the Flies
The Inheritors
The Spire

OLIVER GOLDSMITH
She Stoops to Conquer
The Vicar of Wakefield

ROBERT GRAVES
Goodbye to All That

GRAHAM GREENE
Brighton Rock
The Heart of the Matter
The Power and the Glory

THOMAS HARDY
Far from the Madding Crowd
Jude the Obscure
Selected Poems
Tess of the D'Urbervilles
The Mayor of Casterbridge
The Return of the Native
The Trumpet Major
The Woodlanders
Under the Greenwood Tree

L. P. HARTLEY
The Go-Between
The Shrimp and the Anemone

NATHANIEL HAWTHORNE
The Scarlet Letter

SEAMUS HEANEY
Selected Poems

JOSEPH HELLER
Catch-22

ERNEST HEMINGWAY
A Farewell to Arms
For Whom the Bell Tolls
The African Stories
The Old Man and the Sea

GEORGE HERBERT
Selected Poems

HERMANN HESSE
Steppenwolf

BARRY HINES
Kes

HOMER
The Iliad
The Odyssey

ANTHONY HOPE
The Prisoner of Zenda

GERARD MANLEY HOPKINS
Selected Poems

WILLIAM DEAN HOWELLS
The Rise of Silas Lapham

RICHARD HUGHES
A High Wind in Jamaica

THOMAS HUGHES
Tom Brown's Schooldays

ALDOUS HUXLEY
Brave New World

HENRIK IBSEN
A Doll's House
Ghosts
Hedda Gabler

HENRY JAMES
Daisy Miller
The Ambassadors
The Europeans
The Portrait of a Lady
The Turn of the Screw
Washington Square

SAMUEL JOHNSON
Rasselas

BEN JONSON
The Alchemist
Volpone

JAMES JOYCE
A Portrait of the Artist as a Young Man
Dubliners

JOHN KEATS
Selected Poems

RUDYARD KIPLING
Kim

D. H. LAWRENCE
Sons and Lovers
The Rainbow
Women in Love

CAMARA LAYE
L'Enfant Noir

HARPER LEE
To Kill a Mocking-Bird

LAURIE LEE
Cider with Rosie

THOMAS MANN
Tonio Kröger

CHRISTOPHER MARLOWE
Doctor Faustus
Edward II

ANDREW MARVELL
Selected Poems

W. SOMERSET MAUGHAM
Of Human Bondage
Selected Short Stories

GAVIN MAXWELL
Ring of Bright Water

J. MEADE FALKNER
Moonfleet

HERMAN MELVILLE
Billy Budd
Moby Dick

THOMAS MIDDLETON
Women Beware Women

THOMAS MIDDLETON and WILLIAM ROWLEY
The Changeling

ARTHUR MILLER
Death of a Salesman
The Crucible

JOHN MILTON
Paradise Lost I & II
Paradise Lost IV & IX
Selected Poems

V. S. NAIPAUL
A House for Mr Biswas

SEAN O'CASEY
Juno and the Paycock
The Shadow of a Gunman

GABRIEL OKARA
The Voice

EUGENE O'NEILL
Mourning Becomes Electra

GEORGE ORWELL
Animal Farm
Nineteen Eighty-four

JOHN OSBORNE
Look Back in Anger

WILFRED OWEN
Selected Poems

ALAN PATON
Cry, The Beloved Country

THOMAS LOVE PEACOCK
Nightmare Abbey and *Crotchet Castle*

HAROLD PINTER
The Birthday Party
The Caretaker

PLATO
The Republic

ALEXANDER POPE
Selected Poems

THOMAS PYNCHON
The Crying of Lot 49

SIR WALTER SCOTT
Ivanhoe
Quentin Durward
The Heart of Midlothian
Waverley

PETER SHAFFER
The Royal Hunt of the Sun

WILLIAM SHAKESPEARE
A Midsummer Night's Dream
Antony and Cleopatra
As You Like It
Coriolanus
Cymbeline
Hamlet
Henry IV Part I
Henry IV Part II
Henry V
Julius Caesar
King Lear
Love's Labour Lost
Macbeth
Measure for Measure
Much Ado About Nothing
Othello
Richard II
Richard III
Romeo and Juliet
Sonnets
The Merchant of Venice
The Taming of the Shrew
The Tempest
The Winter's Tale
Troilus and Cressida
Twelfth Night
The Two Gentlemen of Verona

GEORGE BERNARD SHAW
Androcles and the Lion
Arms and the Man
Caesar and Cleopatra
Candida
Major Barbara
Pygmalion
Saint Joan
The Devil's Disciple

MARY SHELLEY
Frankenstein

PERCY BYSSHE SHELLEY
Selected Poems

RICHARD BRINSLEY SHERIDAN
The School for Scandal
The Rivals

WOLE SOYINKA
The Lion and the Jewel
The Road
Three Shorts Plays

EDMUND SPENSER
The Faerie Queene (Book I)

JOHN STEINBECK
Of Mice and Men
The Grapes of Wrath
The Pearl

LAURENCE STERNE
A Sentimental Journey
Tristram Shandy

ROBERT LOUIS STEVENSON
Kidnapped
Treasure Island
Dr Jekyll and Mr Hyde

TOM STOPPARD
Professional Foul
Rosencrantz and Guildenstern are Dead

JONATHAN SWIFT
Gulliver's Travels

JOHN MILLINGTON SYNGE
The Playboy of the Western World

TENNYSON
Selected Poems

W. M. THACKERAY
Vanity Fair

DYLAN THOMAS
Under Milk Wood

EDWARD THOMAS
Selected Poems

FLORA THOMPSON
Lark Rise to Candleford

J. R. R. TOLKIEN
The Hobbit
The Lord of the Rings

CYRIL TOURNEUR
The Revenger's Tragedy

ANTHONY TROLLOPE
Barchester Towers

MARK TWAIN
Huckleberry Finn
Tom Sawyer

JOHN VANBRUGH
The Relapse

VIRGIL
The Aeneid

VOLTAIRE
Candide

EVELYN WAUGH
Decline and Fall
A Handful of Dust

JOHN WEBSTER
The Duchess of Malfi
The White Devil

H. G. WELLS
The History of Mr Polly
The Invisible Man
The War of the Worlds

ARNOLD WESKER
Chips with Everything
Roots

PATRICK WHITE
Voss

OSCAR WILDE
The Importance of Being Earnest

TENNESSEE WILLIAMS
The Glass Menagerie

VIRGINIA WOOLF
Mrs Dalloway
To the Lighthouse

WILLIAM WORDSWORTH
Selected Poems

WILLIAM WYCHERLEY
The Country Wife

W. B. YEATS
Selected Poems

York Handbooks: list of titles

YORK HANDBOOKS form a companion series to York Notes and are designed to meet the wider needs of students of English and related fields. Each volume is a compact study of a given subject area, written by an authority with experience in communicating the essential ideas to students of all levels.